Heroes of Bomber Command

YORKSHIRE

Heroes of Bomber Command

YORKSHIRE

MICHAEL P. WADSWORTH

COUNTRYSIDE BOOKS
NEWBURY BERKSHIRE

First published 2007
© Michael P. Wadsworth 2007

COUNTRYSIDE BOOKS
3 Catherine Road,
Newbury, Berkshire.

To view our complete range of books,
please visit us at
www.countrysidebooks.co.uk

ISBN 978 1 84674 044 2

*Front cover picture shows CO of 78 Squadron, Guy Lawrence,
talking to crews before a Berlin raid – 31 August 1943.*
(Peter Green)

Designed by Peter Davies, Nautilus Design
Produced through MRM Associates Ltd, Reading
Printed by Cambridge University Press

CONTENTS

Acknowledgements

I owe a lot to many people, too numerous to mention, in the research for this book. However, I would like to thank the following, in particular, for their special help: Sandra Badland and Ken for their generous hospitality, and for tracking down important library references for me; Hugh Cawdron for matters relating to W/C David Wilkerson, DSO, DFC, and 578 Squadron, and for permission to use photographs from his excellent book *Based at Burn. Mk II*; Charlie Chapman, DFM, for conversations concerning the chaos of postings within 4 Group, especially before mid-1943; Philip Goodwin for help in the past with matters relating to 104 Squadron, and with wartime life at RAF Driffield; Jim Inward, DFC, for help with matters relating to 35, 76 and 578 Squadrons, including photographs; Harold and Fred Panton for help with matters relating to their late brother, P/O Christopher Panton, and for photographs; Graham Smith for his sage advice, and for help with photographs; Ernest Turtle for help with matters relating to 76 Squadron, including photographs; Geoff Womersley, DSO, DFC, for help in the past with matters relating to 102 Squadron, and with wartime life at RAF Driffield; staff and personnel at the Yorkshire Aviation Museum, Elvington.

Turning to photographs used in this book, the original sources of many of them are now nearly impossible to trace, and I have credited images to the immediate source of supply, unless the name of the original photographer has been ascertained. If I have misappropriated any credits, I apologise, as it was not my intention to do so.

As well as those I have thanked above I am particularly grateful to Peter Green, Graham Pitchfork, Jim Shortland and Andy Thomas (also Ed Dunning, Cy Few, and colleagues at 51 Squadron archive) for sharing with me their vast collections of photographs, and their unrivalled knowledge of the subject. Jim Shortland explored with me the Yorkshire antecedents of 617 Squadron personalities.

I owe a great deal to W.R. Chorley and his magisterial work *Bomber Command Losses 1939-45* (in a number of volumes, Midland Counties Publications *1992-1998*).

Finally I owe a particular debt of gratitude to Anne Smillie-Pearson for word-processing and preparing the manuscript for publication.

Without her help this book could never have got off the ground. She has seen this work through to the very end, and has returned scripts, duly corrected, immediately after submission.

Dedication
This book is dedicated to Margaret Wadsworth, my mother, who played a part in these stirring events, and who lost her aircrew husband, my father, on 27 April 1944; and to Tamara Wadsworth, my wife, who has supported me in an earlier book in my desire to trace my father's footsteps, and in this book to make the bomber war in my native Yorkshire a major area of study.

Abbreviations & Technical Terms

AFC   Air Force Cross
AI   Airborne Interception
A/M   Air Marshal
AOC   Air Officer Commanding
AOC-in-C   Air Officer Commanding-in-Chief
A/P   Aiming Point
ASI   Airspeed Indicator
ATA   Air Transport Auxiliary
A/V/M   Air Vice-Marshal
BEM   British Empire Medal
CAS   Chief of Air Staff
CGM   Conspicuous Gallantry Medal
C in C   Commander in Chief
CO   Commanding Officer
Cpl.   Corporal
DFC   Distinguished Flying Cross
DFM   Distinguished Flying Medal
DSO   Distinguished Service Order
ETA   Estimated Time of Arrival
FIDO   Fog Investigation and Dispersal Operation
F/L   Flight Lieutenant
F/O   Flying Officer
F/S   Flight Sergeant
G/C   Group Captain
Gee   'Ground Electronic Engineering'. An electronic device to guide the aircraft to the target.
GM   George Medal
H2S   A radar aid towards identifying the target (said to come from an earlier code, 'Home Sweet Home', though this is disputed).

HCU	Heavy Conversion Unit
HQ	Headquarters
LAC	Leading Aircraftsman
LNSF	Light Night Striking Force (a force of Pathfinder Mosquito squadrons)
Met.	Meteorological (Aircrew referred to 'Met' as the weather report, or as those who made these reports.)
Oboe	Radar aid to navigation and blind bombing
Op(s)	Operation(s)
ORB	Operations Record Book
OTU	Operational Training Unit
PFF	Pathfinder Force
P/O	Pilot Officer
POW	Prisoner of War
RAAF	Royal Australian Air Force
RAF	Royal Air Force
RCAF	Royal Canadian Air Force
RNAF	Royal Norwegian Air Force
RNZAF	Royal New Zealand Air Force
RT	Radio Transmitter/Transmission
SAAF	South African Air Force
Sgt.	Sergeant
S/L	Squadron Leader
TI	Target Indicator
USAF	United States Air Force (as it is now called)
USAAF	United States Army Air Force (wartime designation)
VC	Victoria Cross
WAAF	Women's Auxiliary Air Force
W/C	Wing Commander
W/O	Warrant Officer

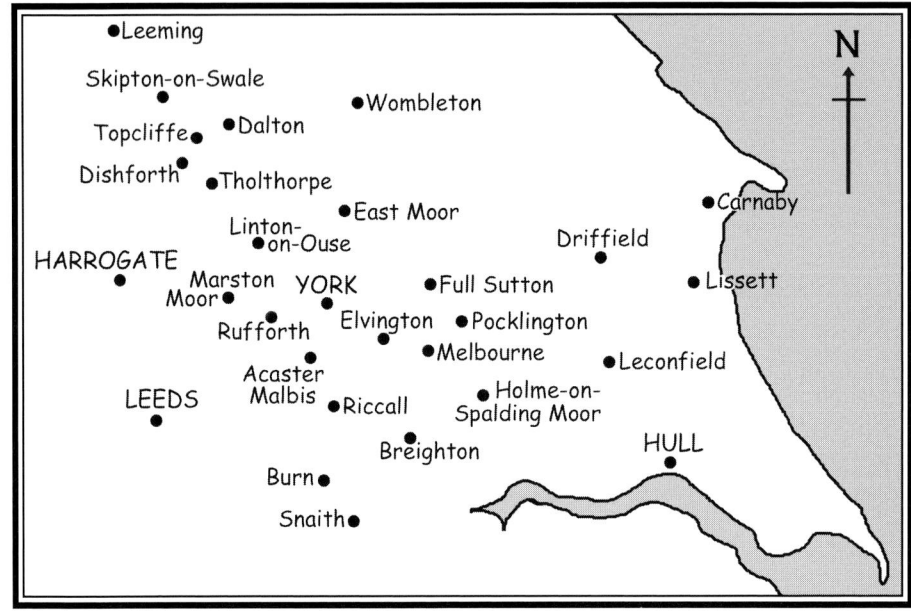

Map of Yorkshire Airfields 1939-1945.

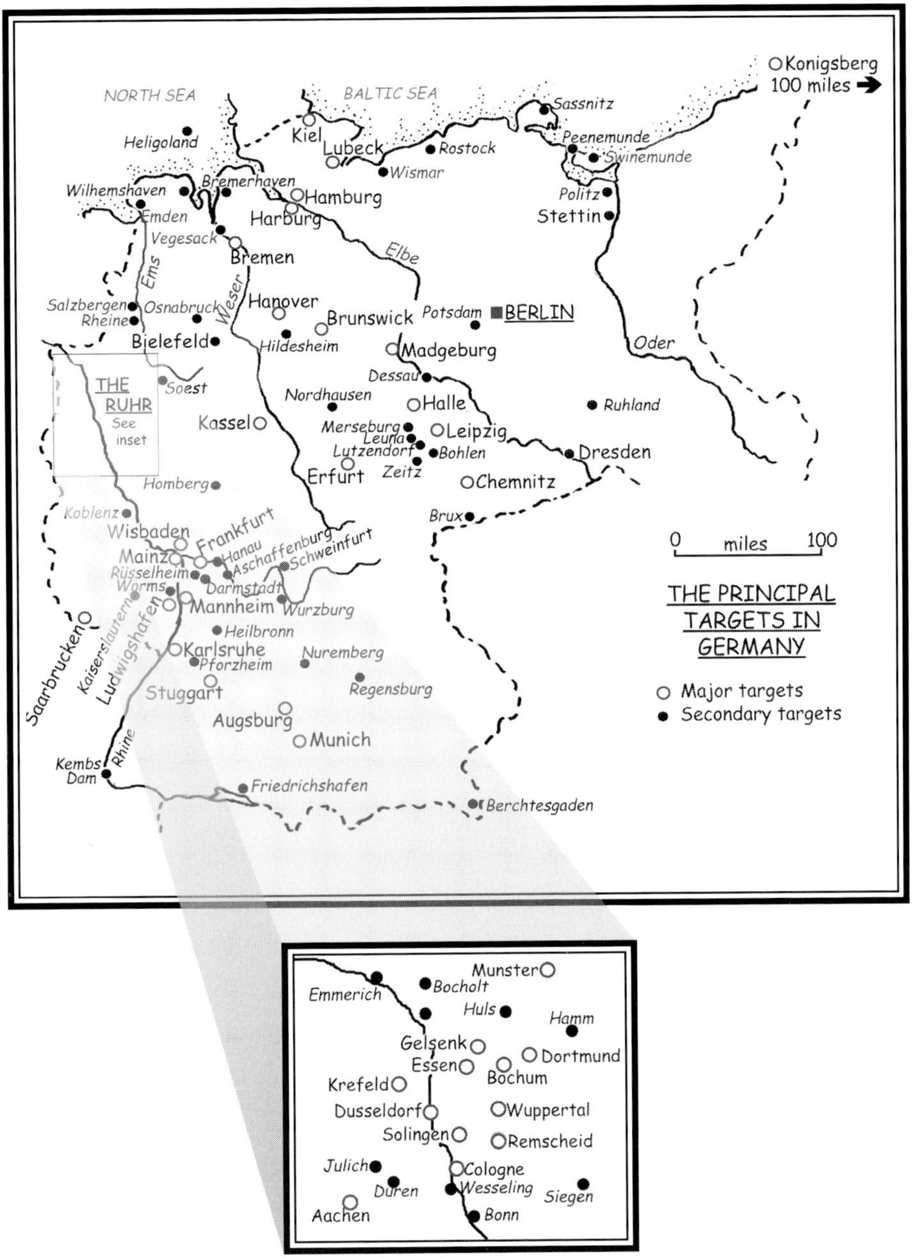

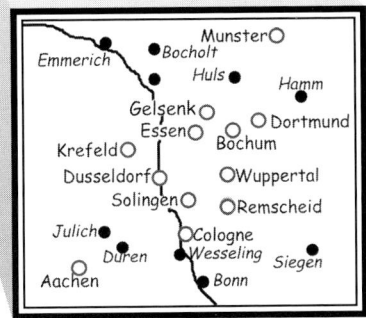

O Konigsberg
100 miles →

NORTH SEA

BALTIC SEA

Heligoland
Kiel
Lubeck
Rostock
Sassnitz
Peenemunde
Swinemunde

Wismar

Wilhemshaven
Bremerhaven
Hamburg
Politz
Emden
Harburg
Stettin

Vegesack
Bremen
Elbe

Salzbergen
Osnabruck
Hanover
Potsdam
■BERLIN
Rheine
Brunswick

Bielefeld
Hildesheim
Madgeburg
Oder

Soest
Dessau
THE
RUHR
See
inset
Nordhausen
Halle
Ruhland

Kassel
Merseburg
Leipzig
Leuna
Erfurt
Lutzendorf
Bohlen
Dresden
Homberg
Zeitz
Chemnitz

Koblenz
Brux
Wisbaden
Frankfurt
Mainz
Hanau
Russelheim
Aschaffenburg
Worms
Schweinfurt
Darmstadt
Mannheim
Wurzburg
Heilbronn
Saarbrucken
Karlsruhe
Nuremberg
Kaiserslautern
Pforzheim
Ludwigshafen
Stuttgart
Regensburg

Augsburg
Munich
Kembs
Dam
Rhine
Friedrichshafen
Berchtesgaden

0 — miles — 100

**THE PRINCIPAL
TARGETS IN
GERMANY**

O Major targets
● Secondary targets

Munster O
Bocholt
Emmerich
Huls
Hamm
Gelsenk O
Essen O
Dortmund
Krefeld O
Bochum
Dusseldorf O
Wuppertal
Solingen O
Remscheid
Julich
Cologne
Duren
Wesseling
Siegen
Aachen
Bonn

Inset map of the Ruhr.

INTRODUCTION

Just over 60 years ago a ferocious and relentless air war was in progress. Night after night young men were flying Halifaxes or Lancasters to devastate the cities of Germany and to squeeze the industrial heart out of the enemy. Some 55,888 aircrew lost their lives, 51% of the total strength of Bomber Command. My interest in Bomber Command and their sacrifices is bound up with my personal story. My father, Flying Officer Philip Wadsworth, was killed in 1944 as a flight engineer with a Pathfinder squadron.

The RAF, despite inadequate preparation in the inter-war years, was created for strategic bombing. The fighter squadrons saved the day in 1940, but it was the strategic bomber from which, it was felt, would come about the means of victory. In these pages we follow the fortunes of the brave men who flew the bombers of 4 Group stationed in the old East Riding of Yorkshire, east of York and north of Hull. By January 1943 the Yorkshire-based squadrons had been joined by 6 Group, the Canadians' own bomber group. Manned almost entirely by the Royal Canadian Air Force, they operated north of Leeds and York, the old North Riding of Yorkshire.

Reading the story of the Yorkshire aircrew, it constantly emerges that theirs was a truly astonishing war to fight. Aircrew could be out with a girl one afternoon in York, Bridlington or Beverley, and the next night locked in dark and uncertain conflict with flak and night fighters all the way to the target, returning, if they were lucky, to empty places at breakfast after debriefing and empty beds in the billets, as missing comrades were swallowed up by the night.

Veterans of the conflict are amazing people, and a joy to talk to. The horror of the bomber war experiences, those far off 'years the locusts have eaten' (to coin a biblical phrase), is forever written in their hearts. They are forever grateful for being alive, and never forget those who made the one-way journey.

This is their story, of the heroes of Bomber Command who made their homes in the Yorkshire landscape. You will find the Yorkshire squadrons contained aircrew from all over the world. Theirs are the stories of brave young men whose exploits, lives and, in all too many cases, deaths have left a powerful torch to bear for everyone who

F/O Philip Wadsworth, the author's father, on his last leave.
(Margaret Wadsworth)

cares about freedom. When they got off the trains with their kit bags and travel warrants at York, Pocklington, Darlington or Driffield, and waited for the transport to the nearby airfield, many would have realised, from the tally of squadron losses which everyone down to the lowliest cook or LAC knew about, that the clock had started to tick for them.

I leave you with some lines from Laurence Binyon's poem *For The Fallen*, lines which come after those well-known ones uttered in the citation every Remembrance Sunday, 'They shall grow not old...'. They evoke images of those gallant aircrew, those heroes of Bomber Command, who left the gramophone on the turntable playing *I don't want to set the world on fire*, while they took off in their Whitleys, Wellingtons, Halifaxes or Lancasters to drop their bombs over half a hundred German and European cities.

> As the stars that shall be bright when we are dust,
> Moving in marches upon the heavenly plain,
> As the stars that are starry in the time of our darkness,
> To the end, to the end, they remain.

Michael G. Woodworth

Chapter 1

From Leaflets
to Bombs

'Whatever people will tell him [the man in the street] the bomber will always get through. The only defence is offence…'

Stanley Baldwin: the House of Commons,
10 November 1932

Many airmen who were to achieve real distinction in subsequent years started their early operations in a Yorkshire setting. Driffield airfield alone, in the early months of the war, had a concentration of talent and distinction: Leonard Cheshire, VC, began his ops with 102 Squadron at Driffield, for instance, as did Melvin Young, who was to take part in the 'bouncing bomb' Dambusters Raid, while Hamish Mahaddie, a sergeant pilot on Driffield's other squadron, 77, would become CO of the Pathfinder Navigation Training Unit down at Warboys in Cambridgeshire. Two Yorkshire pilots – Cyril Barton and Andrew Mynarski – were to be awarded the Victoria Cross, posthumously, for their heroism in the air.

During the Second World War the Yorkshire Wolds (and later on, the moors and dales) would become home to 25 airfields, several to be used in training or by fighter aircraft, but the majority of them as airfields of Bomber Command. On the outbreak of war in September

F/S Hamish Mahaddie and his crew when he was a pilot on 77 Squadron at Driffield.
(Hamish Mahaddie)

1939, however, solid, brick-built aerodromes housed six operational squadrons, all equipped with the redoubtable Armstrong-Whitworth Whitley bomber. The new airfields (built in the previous three to five years) were Driffield, at the foot of the Yorkshire Wolds and home of 77 Squadron and 102 Squadron; Dishforth, adjacent to the Great North Road and east of Ripon, home of 10 Squadron and 78 Squadron; Linton-on-Ouse, north of York, housing 51 Squadron and 58 Squadron; and Leconfield, near Beverley, which was retained briefly on a Care and Maintenance basis before reverting to Fighter Command.

All these squadrons were members of 4 Group, Bomber Command.

In 1936 the RAF had created a functional Command system to replace the old area organization of the Air Defence of Great Britain. Thus 4 Group in the Yorkshire Wolds was founded in 1937. Its HQ was then, rather improbably, at Mildenhall in Suffolk, but was soon relocated to Linton-on-Ouse and then to Heslington Hall in April 1940, just outside York. The first Group Commander was Air Commodore (as he was then) Arthur Harris, but by 1940 the post was held by Air Vice Marshal Cunningham. Air Marshal Sir Edgar Ludlow-Hewitt was succeeded as Commander in Chief of Bomber Command in 1940 by Sir Richard Peirse, who held office until early 1942 and was replaced by the legendary Sir Arthur Harris, whose name became synonymous with Bomber Command.

77 Squadron Whitley Vs at Driffield. (Peter Green)

Staff officers at 4 Group HQ, Heslington Hall, York. Sir Roderick Carr, AOC 4 Group, fourth from left. (51 Squadron archive)

The Whitleys of 4 Group were to take the war to the enemy and their long range, though not their inadequate bomb-carrying capacity, was initially considered sufficient for this. Disastrous encounters with German fighter aircraft in daylight, while attempting to attack enemy shipping in the North Sea, soon made night bombing a prudent necessity. It is no exaggeration to say that the Yorkshire-based squadrons were at the raw edge of developing night-bombing techniques.

Pre-war, the men who flew the Whitleys had been attracted into the RAF by the offer of cadetships at Cranwell, or by the prospect of a short service commission. The creation of the RAF Voluntary Reserve aided this process, as did the University Air Squadrons, which brought Melvin Young and Leonard Cheshire to Driffield. From the very outset of the war the RAF was almost a Commonwealth air force, men from the Dominions coming to this country in quest of a short service commission.

Developing a trade at the RAF Apprentices College at Halton also gave an opportunity to learn to fly. Hamish Mahaddie learned to fly in this way. Men in the pre-war RAF enjoyed the increase in pay which serving as an air gunner or wireless operator in a bomber gave them. The great thing was to fly, and there were many 'air minded' enthusiasts amongst the youth of those days. The problem was that, with the advent of war, training had to be speeded up and navigational proficiency, to highlight

Crews getting ready to board a Whitley for a raid. (Peter Green)

one vital requirement, could only be developed by long and arduous practice. Furthermore, navigation required proficiency in mathematics and, at the very least, a good standard of education. Pilots and navigators had to be a special breed. With the coming of Stirlings and Halifaxes and the need for a flight engineer, ex-Halton entrants were encouraged to volunteer, as were men with technical engineering apprenticeships behind them.

A bomber crew needed an entire arsenal of skills and training. Aircrew were rapidly becoming the most highly trained men in the history of armed warfare. There was never any shortage of volunteers for aircrew even though, as was the case in early 1943, only about 17% of RAF bomber crews could expect to finish a 30-operation tour.

The first night operation took place only hours after war had been declared on 3 September 1939, when ten Whitleys from 51 and 58 Squadrons at Linton-on-Ouse flew to Leconfield to load up with leaflets for what

was known as a 'Nickel' raid, dropping propaganda over Germany. Five nights later on 8 September, S/L Philip Murray of 102 Squadron set out from Driffield on a leaflet-dropping raid and had to bale out over enemy territory when his aircraft suffered engine failure. He and his crew became the first POWs and were taken by their captors to meet Hermann Goering himself, bloated and gloating over them.

Linton-on-Ouse – home of 58 Squadron – from the air. (Peter Green)

On 11 October a report came in to Bomber Command HQ from Air Vice Marshal Cunningham, who wrote: 'The real constant battle is with the weather. The constant struggle at night is to get light onto the target.' The Group Commander predicted 'a never ending struggle to

21

A Whitley V at Leeming – note the heavy camouflage. (Peter Green)

A Whitley V of 102 Squadron, Driffield, having returned from bombing Sylt; pilot S/L Macdonald. (Peter Green)

circumvent the law that we cannot see in the dark'.

The excellent thing from a Group Commander's point of view, however, was the negligible opposition from the Luftwaffe. The real enemy at this stage, as Cunningham had noted, was the weather, in particular the severe icing encountered and the impossibility of maintaining height. Not only would ailerons, rudders and elevators become frozen and jammed, but even inside the cockpit instruments would freeze. Fragile oxygen systems became unusable. And meanwhile St Elmo's Fire or a lightning storm might spell annihilation for an unwary or unprepared crew.

Two of the earliest Distinguished Flying Crosses (DFCs) of the war were awarded to pilots of 102 Squadron, both New Zealanders. F/O Gray and F/O Long brought a severely damaged Whitley back to Driffield on the night of 27/28 November 1939, after it had been nearly torn apart by lightning over the target. F/O Frank 'Lofty' Long, DFC, went on to become Leonard Cheshire's mentor when Cheshire flew second pilot to him during the middle of the next year. Twenty-five-year-old Long was killed on the night of 12/13 March 1941 on a Berlin operation. Over the little village of Denekamp in Holland, his Whitley was attacked by a Messerschmitt and exploded in mid-air. The local people never forgot the incident, and in 2002 a memorial to the crew was unveiled in the Dutch village.

The distances covered on leaflet raids were sometimes vast, as, for example, the Nickel raid on 26 January 1940 when crews had to fly to Villeneuve in France as a forward base against Prague, Vienna and Munich. Conservation of fuel and accuracy of navigation were therefore a problem. On the night of 15/16 March 1940, a Whitley of 77 Squadron was forced to land due to bad weather on what they thought was mainland France, only to find, from the attitude of the locals, that they were on the wrong side of the Franco-German border. Running back to their aircraft and to a quick take-off to avoid the 'hue and cry', they made it to the forward French airfield of Villeneuve with almost no fuel in their tanks.

And still, in this 'phoney war' period, the first actual bombing raid had yet to take place. It came at last in March, after the Germans had bombed the base of the home fleet in Scapa Flow, on the north coast of Scotland. Bombs were scattered over the Isle of Hoy, killing one civilian and wounding seven in the village. So now the gloves were off. On the

Whitley V (102 Squadron) Driffield. (Peter Green)

night of 19/20 March, 30 Whitleys from 4 Group and 20 Hampdens raided the German seaplane base at Hornum on the southern tip of the island of Sylt. Twenty-six Whitleys claimed to have found the target and to have bombed accurately.

The press made much of the contribution of the two Dishforth squadrons, 10 and 51, and stated that the raid had been led by the CO of 10 Squadron, W/C 'Crack Em' Staton. This annoyed the Driffield crews, as a Flight Commander from 102 Squadron, S/L J.C. Macdonald was the first over the target and had in fact bombed first. A party from 102 Squadron entered Dishforth in the early hours of the morning of 22 March and left leaflets under the plates in the Officers' Mess stressing Driffield's premier contribution. The Dishforth crews in reply carried out their own leaflet raid on Driffield. Perhaps, for all the irony, that was a good way for the 'phoney war' to end, although officially and historically it ended when Germany invaded Norway on 8/9 April 1940.

Now offensive raids with real bombs were conducted by the Whitleys of 4 Group against Norwegian airfields and also against oil refineries in the Ruhr. On 14 May the Luftwaffe's indiscriminate terror policy was underlined by a raid on Rotterdam after the German invasion of the Low Countries. The next night Bomber Command sent 108 aircraft to attack more targets deep inside Germany – the start, so some scholars maintain, of the strategic bombing offensive.

Casualties inevitably began to make themselves felt as operations hotted up. Of six aircraft from 102 Squadron at Driffield attacking a synthetic-oil plant at Gelsenkirchen-Buer on the night of 19 May, two (piloted by F/O Longman and F/S Hall) failed to return, while others had narrow escapes. The next night, during a raid by 38 Whitleys of 10 Squadron from Dishforth, two more were shot down, while another two Whitleys were destroyed by enemy ground fire when attacking bridgeheads and enemy troops the night after, with the crew of one, captained by P/O Geoff Womersley of 102 Squadron, baling out near Metz.

Geoff Womersley was thus spared for an astonishing wartime career, ending up as Station Commander of the Pathfinder Force RAF station at Gransden Lodge in Bedfordshire. He flew operationally Whitleys, Wellingtons, Lancasters and Mosquitos, and had a long and distinguished war. When, at the outbreak of hostilities, all leave was stopped, Geoff Womersley and his fiancée were married in Driffield, and rented a house in York Road just further along from the house in which I was born. So P/O Womersley started his distinguished

W/C (later G/C) Geoff Womersley, CO of 139 Squadron (PFF) and Station Commander of Gransden Lodge (PFF). Started off as a young P/O of 102 Squadron at Driffield. (Geoff Womersley)

Whitley V of 78 Squadron at Dishforth. (Peter Green)

operational career in Driffield, and also embarked there on a long and happy married life.

On the night of 27 May 1940, 36 Whitleys from 4 Group were sent to the Ruhr marshalling yards. One pilot of 10 Squadron, P/O Warren, battled against a severe electrical storm which sent his compass heading and navigational courses all adrift, so that disorientated, he mistook the Thames for the Rhine and bombed Bassingbourn airfield. Fortunately there were no casualties and minimal damage. P/O Warren had to go back to being second pilot again for a while and was dubbed 'Baron von Warren' by fellow aircrew!

The declaration of war by Italy at midnight, 10 June 1940, was the spur for a bombing raid on Italian targets on the next night. Whitleys of 4 Group were involved here, with aircraft from 10, 51 and 58 squadrons flying to Guernsey airport and taking off from that forward base, while 77 and 102 squadrons used Jersey. Specific targets were

the Fiat aero-engine and motor works in Turin, or as an alternative the Ansaldo factories in Genoa. This was the greatest challenge to face the Whitley crews so far. It was a struggle, for a start, to cope with the short runways of Jersey and Guernsey, and from the Channel Islands to Turin is approximately 1,100 miles. But the storms harassing the Whitleys as they attempted to clear the Alps were deadly and memorable.

Bill Jacobs, wireless operator in a 102 Squadron aircraft, recalled that his skipper had to abort this trip as icing made the climb over the Alps prohibitive: 'Our poor old Whitley was not up to the task.' The raid, though not achieving much damage, was deeply symbolic for 4 Group and for the RAF. The enemy, now, could be reached and attacked.

Early in 1940, 78 Squadron at Dishforth became fully operational, attacking the Ruhr marshalling yards with four Whitleys. Industrial plants that made a difference to Germany's ability to wage war were bombed remorselessly, including aircraft assembly plants at Wenzendorf and Wismar, and the marshalling yards at Soest.

The Luftwaffe's response to all these Whitley raids, apart from their

seeking out fighter airfields, reached the bomber stations on 15 August 1940 with a blistering attack on Driffield aerodrome which, in terms of a German approach across the North Sea, is the most easterly in Britain. Shortly after 1 pm a force of 50 Junkers Ju 88s flew from their base of Aalborg in Denmark over the coast just south of Bridlington and attacked Driffield. A resident just opposite our family home stood at the door and waved a teapot in defiance at the aircraft, but was instructed to go to the shelter, as both our houses were quite near to the airfield and German aircrew were indiscriminate in the use of machine guns.

From the German point of view it was an effective raid, the heaviest of the war on an RAF bomber station. Thirteen people were killed, including a civilian employee of the station, seven members of the RAF (and the first WAAF of the war), and five members of the East Yorkshire Regiment. Twelve Whitleys were destroyed on the ground and the aerodrome was dive-bombed and strafed. A Vickers .303 machine gun, from its vantage point on the airfield's water tower, gave brisk retaliation. Spitfires, scrambled from Leconfield and Church Fenton, shot down seven German aircraft, with three badly damaged.

After the bombing of the airfield, an effort was made to conduct 'business as usual'. Nineteen aircraft from Driffield took part in a raid on the Daimler-Benz factory at Stuttgart on the night of 24/25 August 1940. The end of the month, however, saw the two Driffield squadrons seeking a new location, while the airfield was closed for repairs. All remaining aircraft and personnel of 102 Squadron moved to RAF Leeming, while RAF Topcliffe, a later part of the pre-war RAF expansion phase with 1930s brick-built hangars, and which had only just opened, was used for the dispersal of 102's aircraft. Two days later, on 28 August, 77 Squadron moved to Linton-on-Ouse, their aircraft to Tholthorpe, and their maintenance flight to Topcliffe. RAF Tholthorpe was another newly opened airfield, a grass-field satellite to Linton-on-Ouse, close to the town of Easingwold.

This moving about and frequent relocating is very largely the story of 4 Group, Bomber Command until about 1943, after which more settled conditions prevailed. However, the constant moving never – or hardly ever – got in the way of the aircraft operating on every possible occasion and taking the war to the enemy. The bomber force was only at the fledgling stage. It was to become Britain's supreme instrument of war.

Chapter 2

Oil Plants and German Cities

I love to fly a Whitley Five
And put her in a power dive,
And pull her out at One-nine-five.
It's foolish but it's fun.

Aircrew song, derived from 51 Squadron

The first German bombs fell on central London on 24 August 1940. The next night Churchill and the War Cabinet retaliated by ordering the bombing of Berlin. Once again, as in the case of the Italian raids, the consequences of this first Berlin raid were symbolic rather than effective.

One hundred and three aircraft from 3, 4 and 5 Groups were sent out on the night of 25/26 August, some to Berlin and others to bomb Bremen, Cologne and Hamm. All the Whitleys of 4 Group returned safely. According to Sergeant Jock Hill, a wireless operator of 78 Squadron, the trip took 9 hours and 40 minutes, so that the aircraft were at the limit of their fuel capacity. One of the Hampdens from 50 Squadron at Lindholme (then in 5 Group) came down in the sea within sight of Scarborough but P/O George Potts and his crew were rescued by the local fishermen. P/O Wawne, from the same squadron, unfortunately landed his Hampden in southern Germany after leaving

Bombing up a Wellington. (Peter Green)

Bombing up a Wellington. (Peter Green)

Berlin, believing he was in Scotland!

After the raid, only 29 crews claimed to have bombed the target. Yet British aircraft had penetrated to the very heart of the Reich and it had a deep psychological effect on the German people.

Italian targets continued to be sought out by the Whitleys of the Yorkshire squadrons, although such long-distance flights, including the

Bombing up a Wellington – rear turret and ammunition. (Peter Green)

hop over the Alps, were supremely testing. On the night of 2 September 1940, S/L Bartlett and F/S Moore of 58 Squadron, Linton-on-Ouse, both had to ditch when they returned to these shores, as they had run out of fuel. S/L Bartlett's crew managed to reach Margate in their dinghy, and the crew of F/S Moore were picked up by a ship when they came down into the sea off Aldeburgh on the Suffolk coast.

A number of Berlin raids were made in September 1940 in retaliation for the continuing and terrible German blitz on Britain. But the prime

Ground crew around rear turret of Whitley V special, 58 Squadron, Linton-on-Ouse.
(Peter Green)

concern in directives sent from the War Cabinet, was upon the bombing of the barges massed at the Channel ports, awaiting word that Goering's Luftwaffe had cleared the way for the invasion of Great Britain to begin. Whitleys from Dishforth, Leeming and Topcliffe made frequent raids on the shipping and transport assembled at Calais, Boulogne, Le Havre, Lorient and Antwerp. In one heavy attack on Antwerp on 14 September, Whitleys from 10, 51 and 78 squadrons inflicted damage on transport and shipping, and blew up an ammunition train – by 19 September the Germans had lost over 200 invasion barges.

German retaliation now overtook one of the squadrons that had been displaced from Driffield by the summer bombing. A Luftwaffe intruder aircraft, a Junkers Ju 88, intercepted and brought down a Whitley of 102 Squadron that had just taken off from Tholthorpe on a raid to Berlin. Two crew members were killed, including a New Zealander, Sgt Scouler, and three were badly injured. Many New Zealanders, after training together at Ohakea and travelling to Britain in one of the big troop ships, were paying the supreme penalty, one by one. Such enemy intruder raids continued from the autumn into the winter of 1940.

There was a much needed honour for 102 Squadron on the night of 12/13 November 1940, when P/O Leonard Cheshire tackled a hideously difficult situation on a raid to Cologne. Over the marshalling yards of the city a series of violent explosions sent his Whitley plummeting earthwards. There was black smoke in the cockpit and fire in the fuselage. Cheshire fought with the controls and gradually regained mastery. The fires were put out, although a large gaping hole was left in the fuselage, and the bombs were successfully dropped on the marshalling yards. Despite losing all his maps in the fire, he made a successful landfall on the English coast. Cheshire received the DSO for this exploit, while the wireless operator, Sgt Davidson, who had stayed at his post and fought the flames, received the DFM. Temporarily blinded in the incident, he later recovered his sight.

Leonard Cheshire went on to become one of the most famous airmen of the Second World War, earning a Victoria Cross in 1944 when he had completed 100 bombing missions over Germany. Born in 1917, he had joined the RAF at the beginning of the war, having served in the Oxford University Air Squadron. In June 1940 he was posted to Driffield and 102 Squadron, and took part in a series of offensive operations against tactical targets such as enemy troop concentrations and bridgeheads,

G/C Leonard Cheshire, VC – a young pilot officer at Driffield with 102 Squadron. He was CO of 76 Squadron and Station Commander of Marston Moor, and CO of 617 Squadron, awarded the VC in 1944. (via Jim Shortland)

as events moved inexorably towards the evacuation of British troops from the beaches of Dunkirk. By November 1943 he was commander of 617 Squadron and developing the low-level marking techniques that would be so important to the effectiveness of bombing missions over Germany. In 1945 he was the official British observer when the atom bomb was dropped on Nagasaki in Japan, bringing the war in the Far East to an end, and for the rest of his life he worked for world peace and nuclear disarmament. In 1991 he was created Baron Cheshire, and he died on 31 July 1992.

At the same time as his eventful trip to Cologne, an aircraft was introduced into operational service in 4 Group with which Cheshire himself was to have much to do in the future. No 35 Squadron collected its first Halifax Mark I on 13 November at Boscombe Down and moved to RAF Leeming and 4 Group a week later. In December 1940, they moved to Linton-on-Ouse, and the following year the new Halifax flew its first mission. The Halifax Mark I was the first four-engined heavy bomber to fly operationally in 4 Group.

Leeming with a Whitley V of 10 Squadron. (Peter Green)

A Halifax over an industrial target, possibly the oil target of Wanne-Eickel.
(Graham Pitchfork)

Throughout all these comings and goings, the highest authorities were worried about the effectiveness of Bomber Command operations, and this uncertainty was to continue until the appointment of Arthur Harris as Commander-in-Chief in February 1942. In October 1940 Churchill had insisted that 'a whole hearted effort shall be made to cart a large number of bombs into Germany', but the next month, on 12 November, the redoubtable W/C Kelly Barnes reached the shocking conclusion that only 35% of all bombers sent out were reaching their primary target. His report had official status, as the Wing Commander was the Chairman of a Group Navigation Officers Conference at Bomber Command HQ.

Meanwhile, what the Air Ministry called 'normal' bombing of

Germany continued throughout October, November and December 1940. Between November and the end of December, therefore, there were five attacks on Berlin, and the oil targets received ever-increasing punishment – Ruhlen, Gelsenkirchen and Merseburg – when the intention was to hit specific targets and cut off Germany's source of supply.

But already a new idea was being advanced which made this seem the tactic of a bygone age. Prompted by the stern warnings being delivered by navigational pundits such as Kelly Barnes, the notion of attacking specific industrial targets was being abandoned, and a policy introduced which was more in line with Chief of the Air Staff Sir Charles Portal's long-held convictions. Now German industrial towns were to be attacked in strength, 'without specific objective other than as an industrial centre'.

On 16 December 1940, a month after the Luftwaffe's wounding attack on Coventry (14/15 November) which had practically reduced the city to rubble, Mannheim was selected for similar treatment. The centre of the town itself was the target of the largest force yet sent out by Bomber Command, 130 aircraft in all. F/O Leonard Cheshire, by this time captain of his own Whitley, described the scene as 'literally a fire from end to end'. Fourteen Wellingtons flew on ahead with incendiaries only, to light fires which would function as markers for the oncoming wave, a rudimentary 'pathfinder' method and one the Germans had introduced at Coventry. Two Hampdens and one Blenheim failed to return.

Following the raid, the Commander-in-Chief, Sir Richard Peirse, signalled his congratulations to all units, but was disappointed to learn when the Photographic Reconnaissance Unit had done its work that though 'considerable damage' had been done, photographs still showed up 'a wide dispersal' of attack.

Meanwhile, it was felt that the pressure on Italian targets must be kept up and in November 1940 the Fiat works in Turin was bombed. Sgt Douglas Mourton of 102 Squadron later recalled that they flew to an advanced base at Horsham St Faith, near Norwich, had a meal and refuelled and then set off for Italy. The target was covered in cloud, although the bombs were dropping. On the return leg, with his fuel well nigh drained, Mourton's pilot, Sgt Rix, and crew were forced to bale out over Midhurst in Sussex.

Another aircraft force-landed near Brighton, while a third ditched in the sea off Plymouth. This last was piloted by F/O Melvin Young, Leonard Cheshire's Oxford contemporary from the University Air Squadron. He was rescued a few hours later and earned the nickname 'Dinghy'. Young was a Californian who had joined the RAF Voluntary Reserve in August 1939 and began his service with 102 Squadron in June 1940, at the same time as Cheshire. He, too, had a distinguished war, earning a DFC in May 1941 after 28 'ops' and being made Squadron Leader in June 1942. He was killed on the Dambusters raid on 17 May 1943, flying with 617 Squadron.

Melvin Young ('Dinghy' Young), pilot with Leonard Cheshire on 102 Squadron, Driffield. Of Anglo-American background, he was killed on the Dams Raid. (via Jim Shortland)

No 102 was maintaining its reputation as a 'chop' squadron – RAF slang for a squadron with too many casualties 'chopped' from the records. On returning from Duisburg on the night of 20/21 November 1940, two nights before the Turin trip, W/C S.R. Groom (who had become CO of 102 Squadron in the Driffield period) and his crew crashed into the North Sea, and on the evening of 2 January 1941, Desmond Coutts and his crew were likewise shot down into the water. The death of S/L Florigny, one of the flight commanders, on a trip to Cologne was particularly poignant. His Whitley had to ditch on the return journey, off Cromer. The tail gunner, Richard Rivaz (who finished the war as S/L Rivaz, DFC) describes in his book *Tail Gunner* how Florigny was last seen standing on the downed aircraft's fuselage, unable to reach the dinghy, blown away from the Whitley by strong winds. The other four members of the crew were saved. The tragedy was compounded by the fact that his brother was killed the same night in a 10 Squadron Whitley, flying from Leeming.

During March 1941, raids continued on U-boat yards, a necessary diversion from orthodox RAF oil targets because of the threat the submarines posed to Allied shipping in the Atlantic. So 4 Group Whitleys visited Bremen, Wilhelmshaven and Lorient, not to mention the harbour of Brest where the German battle cruisers, *Scharnhorst* and *Gneisenau* ('Salmon and Gluckstein', the aircrew called them) were seeking sanctuary and protection. These two great ships continued to be a particular threat to the convoys using the essential trade routes that kept Britain fighting.

When the weather would not permit precision raids like these it was back to oil targets, although attacks on industrial locations to cause maximum civilian disruption would soon come to supersede all others. In June and July 1941, 13 Whitleys would be lost and 40 crew members killed or missing, with a further 18 prisoners of war. A 102 Squadron song, composed at this time, celebrated its low fortunes with a kind of gallows humour:

> And when you come to 102
> And think that you will get right through
> There's many a fool who thought like you,
> It's suicide, but it's fun.

It was on 10 March 1941 that 35 Squadron made its first operational foray with the new Halifax, when seven aircraft attacked Le Havre docks. First off and first to drop his bomb was W/C Ray Collings, the future Pathfinder Commander of 156 Squadron. The Halifaxes raided U-boat yards at Hamburg the next night.

Early in 1941, on 10 February, the first airborne operation of the war was mounted in Bomber Command aircraft. By this time two Whitley squadrons, 51 and 78, were stationed at Dishforth. A new force known as X Troop, No 11 SAS Battalion, was briefed to strike at an aqueduct spanning the River Tragino in Campagna, Southern Italy, and the raid was to be mounted from Malta. After the paratroops had blown up the aqueduct they were supposed to be picked up by a submarine at a rendezvous point 50 miles away on the west coast of Italy. The Whitleys were adapted for the dropping of paratroops, and were under the command of W/C Willie Tait. One of the aircraft got into difficulties, and had to crash land – the crew were captured, and

Battle-damaged rear turret of a Whitley V of 51 Squadron, Dishforth. (Peter Green)

ultimately so were the SAS soldiers. Damage was done to the aqueduct, but the operation was a gallant failure.

A more successful airborne operation would be mounted a year later, 27/28 February 1942, by Whitleys of 51 Squadron, led this time by their CO, W/C Percy Pickard, DSO. Vital equipment from the Wurzburg radar installation at Bruneval, close to Le Havre, was brought out by the paratroopers, to be returned to England and examination by our scientists. King George VI and Queen Elizabeth later visited Dishforth to congratulate Pickard personally, who received a Bar to his DSO.

Pickard gained national fame when he took a break from operations and appeared as the pilot of Wellington 'F for Freddie' in the hugely popular feature film *Target for Tonight*. He became one of the legendary wartime bomber heroes, flying covert sorties while with 161 Squadron for the Special Operations Executive (SOE), dropping supplies and agents in Occupied Europe. Sadly he did not survive the war, being killed in his Mosquito leading the Amiens prison raid on 18 February 1944, when over 250 prisoners were liberated from the Gestapo. Typically, when he came under attack by two Focke Wulf Fw 190s and was shot down, he was attempting to check on survivors from a fellow Mosquito below him.

Chapter 3

New Squadrons, New Airfields

Ops in a Wimpy, ops in a Wimpy,
Who'll come on ops in a Wimpy with me?
And I sang as the ack-ack worked so patiently,
Who'll come on ops in a Wimpy with me?

Popular aircrew song, to tune of Waltzing Matilda

By early April 1941 a second Halifax squadron, No 76, had moved to Linton-on-Ouse with W/C S.O. Bufton as Commanding Officer, only to move again in June to Middleton St George, a new base just across the Yorkshire border in County Durham. They shared Middleton briefly with 78 Squadron, which had arrived from Dishforth with 16 Whitley Mark Vs, but it was not long before 78 Squadron moved to Croft, recently brought into use as a satellite airfield. There it began conversion to the Halifax. In July, W/C J.B. ('Willie') Tait came to Middleton as CO of 76 Squadron.

Willie Tait had had an adventurous few months prior to his appointment. In February he had been in command of the Whitley paratroop operation from Malta. On 15/16 April, while Flight Commander of 'A' Flight, 35 Squadron, he had led the squadron's five

Halifaxes, one of which was piloted by Leonard Cheshire, in a raid on Kiel.

The raid was moderately successful and some damage was done. One Whitley, piloted by Sgt Wally Lashbrook, had to crash land a mile from Linton but none of the crew were lost, although the broken fuselage of the crashed aircraft might suggest otherwise to an uninformed observer. Willie Tait (then Squadron Leader) was awarded a well deserved DSO to add to his DFC. Kiel was always a heavily defended target, and it was remarkable that Tait brought all his Halifaxes back.

The 30th June saw a daylight attack on Brest, the first 'daylight' 35 Squadron had done. There were two waves of Halifaxes, the first led again by Willie Tait. A significant amount of damage was done to docks and shipping.

Close formation flying was observed both to and from the target. One aircraft, piloted by F/O Robert Owen, found it difficult to rejoin the formation on leaving the target due to an attack by four enemy aircraft. One of the gunners was severely wounded and despite attempts to save him, he died on the journey home. Sgt Douglas Hogg was commended for coping with the fighter and defending the aircraft against more grievous attacks. After the Halifax reached welcome cloud cover, and in spite of future potential attacks by fighters, Hogg calmly used some spare wire to replace damaged leads in the wireless set. Despite the repeated and prolonged attacks by the Luftwaffe, all the 35 Squadron aircraft on this raid made it back to Linton-on-Ouse, except for one, piloted by a New Zealander, F/L Thomas Robinson. One member of his crew survived to become a POW. Word had got around that something remarkable had happened over Brest that day, so that when the Halifaxes limped back to their home airfield, almost the entire station turned out to greet them.

Among those decorated after this action, S/L Willie Tait received a Bar to his DSO. Before the end of the war, by which time he commanded 617 Squadron, he had received a third Bar (one of only a handful of RAF officers to be honoured in this way). Like Cheshire, with whom he was often thrown together, Tait was a meteoric figure, concerned to work things out to make them happen. Both of them were reflective men of action, highly intelligent airmen, and both played a remarkable part in 4 Group operations in Yorkshire before leaving to command, at different phases of the war, 617 Squadron. Sgt Hogg, the imperturbable gunner and wireless operator, received the DFM.

Meanwhile there had been a general shake down at Driffield too. Reopened as a bomber station after the disaster of August 1940 and an interlude as a fighter station, the spring of 1941 saw Driffield brought back into 4 Group, Bomber Command. No 104 Squadron was reformed there on 1 April with S/L D.B.G. Tomlinson as CO. It was equipped with the Wellington Mark II, powered by Rolls-Royce Merlin X engines, just like the Whitley V. Thus the aircraft's performance was stepped up and the Wellington, furthermore, was modified to carry

'Moonshine' gremlin painted on side of the Wellington II. (Chaz Bowyer)

Wellington II of 405 (RCAF) Squadron at Driffield, summer 1941. (Peter Green)

the 4,000 lb 'cookie' bomb. Wellingtons were affectionately known as 'Wimpys' after J. Wellington Wimpy, a cartoon character of the day.

By 23 April a second bomber squadron, also equipped with Wellington Mark IIs, had made its home at Driffield. This was 405 (Vancouver) Squadron, the very first Royal Canadian Air Force (RCAF) bomber squadron to form overseas, and the precursor of 6 Canadian Group that would come into existence on 1 January 1943 and occupy most of the North Yorkshire aerodromes.

The first operational sortie for the Canadian squadron was a raid on the marshalling yards at Schwerte near Dortmund in the Ruhr Valley, or 'Happy Valley' as aircrew called it. One Canadian Wellington had to return to Driffield with engine trouble but the rest proceeded to the target with 80 other aircraft, all Whitleys.

On 16/17 June 1941, 405 Squadron suffered the RCAF's first casualty, flying from the recently completed airfield at Pocklington to Cologne. One Wellington, piloted by Sgt W.F. MacGregor, came down into the North Sea with the loss of all crew.

Three days later, 405 Squadron moved in its entirety from Driffield to Pocklington. Driffield was still equipped with grass runways, which quite clearly could not accommodate the two Wellington squadrons. So 104 Squadron was left, to fly 373 Wellington sorties from Driffield and to lose 13 aircraft.

On one raid from Driffield, a daylight attack by 100 aircraft on the battlecruiser *Gneisenau*, old 'Gluckstein', still in dock at Brest, a Wellington piloted by S/L Budden was cut up by enemy aircraft. One of the Spitfires in the escort, flown by that redoubtable Yorkshireman, Ginger Lacey, thought that she looked 'like a flying birdcage', with her geodetic structure laid bare to the heavens (all the fabric was stripped away from wings to rear turret). Harry Budden got her down in a dramatic emergency landing at Exeter airport, with no flaps, damaged ailerons and no wheels. He was awarded an immediate DSO, his co-pilot, P/O R.H. Hutton, received the DFC, and Sgt Armstrong, who had stayed at his post in the turret, though wounded, the DFM. On 12/13 August 1941 Harry went off to bomb Berlin, and became a prisoner of war with the rest of his crew.

Some airfields, with the comings and goings of two or more squadrons, could not accommodate all the aircrew and other personnel so they were billeted nearby. One crew from Driffield was billeted at the Rectory at Bainton, a village near to the aerodrome and another at Wansford

Halifax Mk I at Middleton St George, 1941. (Peter Green)

Rectory, not far from the Trout Inn. One young man, Philip Goodwin, came to Driffield in April 1941 as a pilot with 104 Squadron, flying Wellingtons. He was billeted at the Mill House, King's Mill. It was not far from the aerodrome, and he flew 20 operations while here. Scheduled for the overseas echelon of 104 Squadron, he was posted to Malta thereafter. Eventually he joined my father's squadron, 156 Pathfinder, as a Squadron Leader at Upwood, and was shot down and became a POW on the ill fated Nuremburg raid.

There were two main watering holes for Driffield crews, the Bell Hotel in the very centre of town, an old Georgian coaching inn which had an historic reputation and was popular with 'fishing gents', and the Buck Hotel, 'Hangar No 6' as it came to be called, where all the girls used to go to meet aircrew. There was an indefinable glamour about aircrew.

Leeming 1941, a Whitley V being serviced. (Peter Green)

Whitley V, 10 Squadron, in flight. (Peter Green)

Ops Room – Leeming, August 1941. (Peter Green)

Aircraft were being lost all over Bomber Command as the bomber offensive gathered momentum. On the night of 18/19 June 1941, 10 Squadron lost one aircraft, with the lives of five men, on a raid on Bremen, while a raid on the same target nine days later accounted for another 15 men. High-speed launches from Grimsby saved many lives that would otherwise have been claimed by the North Sea,

That second Bremen raid, on the night of 27/28 June 1941, turned out to be a disastrous night for 4 Group's Whitley Vs. Topcliffe lost seven Whitleys, three from 77 Squadron and four from 102 Squadron. One

pilot who died on this raid was S/L McArthur, DFM, who had been with 102 Squadron as a Sergeant Pilot and had flown from Driffield on the first operation of the war.

The last Whitley from 10 Squadron was lost on 12 December 1941 when, returning from Cologne, it crashed on high ground near Pateley Bridge. Happily only one of the stricken crew was killed. The squadron thereafter turned to converting to Halifax IIs, flying for the first time to attack the battlecruisers *Scharnhorst* and *Gneisenau* at Brest on 18 December.

No 51 Squadron had a vigorous and exciting six months as the sole squadron now based at Dishforth. On the way back from Brest a Whitley was shot down by a Hurricane over Dorset (the 'friendly fire' incidents were becoming ever more frequent), and there were more losses in raids on Frankfurt, Cologne and Berlin in August and September. The last Whitley operation by 51 Squadron from Dishforth was to be in April 1942. By the spring of that year this reliable old workhorse had been withdrawn from service, apart from glider towing, but not until after the '1,000 bomber' raids when every available aircraft was pressed into service.

On 26 July 1941 an important change of command occurred. Air Vice Marshal Cunningham, who had been 4 Group's commander since before war broke out, was replaced by Air Vice Marshal 'Roddy' Carr, a tough New Zealander who would be commander of 4 Group to the end of the war. Cunningham was posted to the Middle East to command the Desert Air Force, which he did with great success.

There was also a shake-up among the topmost ranks of Bomber Command, after a report based on the detailed analysis of photographs taken on raids at night during June and July 1941, demonstrated beyond doubt that most bombers were not even finding their target. Only a third were dropping their bombs within five miles of the designated aiming point, while in 'Happy Valley', the Ruhr, only one in ten did so. Churchill and the War Cabinet reacted to this by accelerating the development of navigational aids, and by preparing for the expansion of Bomber Command to a strength of 4,000 aircraft.

Meanwhile the Halifax was undergoing teething troubles. Some Mark I Halifaxes were bursting into flames when the undercarriage was lowered. One of the new Halifax squadron commanders, W/C Bufton of 76 Squadron determined to sort this out with Handley Page, and had signal success, but all this was in the midst of and in spite of Bomber Command's relentless schedule. The same troubles were felt in Leonard Cheshire's squadron, No 35 at Linton-on-Ouse.

Leonard Cheshire's younger brother, Christopher, now joined 76 Squadron at Dishforth, and was with it when it moved to Middleton St George. On a trip to Berlin on 12/13 August 1941 in which Leonard also took part, flying from Linton, Christopher's Halifax was shot down. Five of the crew baled out, among them Christopher, but the rear gunner, Sgt Woods and the front gunner, Sgt Niven, were killed.

A raid by 169 Whitley aircraft (including 42 Whitleys from 4 Group) on Berlin on the night of 7/8 November 1941 had an almost seismic effect on bombing hopes and expectations. For the Berlin raid was part of a larger, more thoroughgoing offensive in which a further 200 aircraft were also sent out to Cologne, Essen, Mannheim, and some of the Channel ports. The raid in all its variety and boldness was planned and executed in the face of a weather forecast of thunderstorms, severe icing, hail and cloud.

Johnny Fauquier, 'B' Flight commander of 405 Squadron at Pocklington, flew back from Berlin in a Wellington heavily damaged by flak, in the teeth of a 70 mph headwind that diminished inexorably their fuel reserves. The weather was described in the report based on the experiences of the crews who flew from Pocklington as 'Bad, 10/10 cloud with few breaks'. The crew that went missing from Pocklington, piloted by Sgt Hassan, sent a signal to base at 02.23 hours, 'Operation completed', but nothing more was heard of them. They were, in all probability, swallowed by the night and the sea, with the destructive power of the ice building up all the time on the wings of the aircraft.

The Whitleys on the Berlin raid took up to eleven hours to complete the operation. A 78 Squadron crew, piloted by Sgt Lloyd-Jones, landed at Coltishall with only two gallons of fuel in the tanks, after a desperate flight fighting the controls and jettisoning all kinds of impedimenta including the four Browning machine guns from the rear turret. Two

Whitleys were missing from Dishforth and 51 Squadron, and three from 102 Squadron at Topcliffe.

It is extremely revealing that several aircraft called for a QDM at a significant time ('QDM' is wireless operator's telegraphese for 'What is my magnetic course to steer to base?'). Men from 76 Squadron at Middleton St George speak of their compasses freezing on that night. Sgt Matthews, missing from Topcliffe and 102 Squadron, called for a course at 07.26 hours, a timing which reflects the sad fact that he was on his way back and yet he doubtless fell into the sea when he could not navigate home and his tanks were drained to the last drop.

P/O Graham Mandeno of 58 Squadron, from Linton-on-Ouse, had his Whitley damaged by flak and fire over Emden. Nevertheless, says the record, 'he continued to return safely'. This is a classic understatement, and the beginning of a reputation that followed 'Mandy' (his aircrew nickname) throughout his operational career. One day when there were two aircraft out on the hard standings, both of which Mandy had brought back on successive nights with improbable degrees of battle damage, someone commented in another sublime understatement, 'Mandy bent those kites a bit'.

Halifax Mk II in flight. This was the aircraft of Leonard Cheshire's brother, Christopher, who was shot down and became a POW 13 August 1941.
(51 Squadron archive)

The Berlin raid was the greatest effort by Bomber Command so far, and it ended disastrously; 37 aircraft in total were lost, twelve from 4 Group, including nine Whitleys. The next major raid on the city would not be until January 1943, and the War Cabinet ordered a severe reduction of Bomber Command operations until the end of the winter. The entire future of Bomber Command was being called into question.

On 18 December 1941 the Halifax squadrons of 4 Group – six Halifaxes from each squadron – were called upon to mount a daylight attack on the *Scharnhorst* and *Gneisenau* in Brest. The results were encouraging, with black smoke rising from the *Gneisenau*. W/C Basil Robinson, CO of 35 Squadron, was the only one of the Halifaxes in the mixed force to be thought lost. Instead, he achieved the distinction on this raid of being the first Halifax to ditch successfully, although this claim was challenged just after the war by S/L Williams, a former POW, who claimed he had also ditched with success on 24 July 1941.

The rear gunner of Robinson's aircraft, F/L Rivaz, broke a bone in his foot as a result of the violent impact when the Halifax hit the water. It was his second ditching and, like Melvyn Young, he would forever be associated with the name 'Dinghy'. The dinghy inflated and the crew, one by one, stepped from the plane into it, except for 'Robbie', who went back into the aircraft to retrieve his pipe, which he clasped in his teeth, unlit and sticking out of his oxygen mask, whenever he went on operations.

In the night the crew were rescued by a large Royal Navy torpedo boat, and when they returned by train the next day they were met on York station by half the squadron on the platform singing 'The Wingco's in the drink'. W/C Robinson had indeed demonstrated his skill and courage. The aircraft was afloat after ditching for 20 minutes, which is why he had time and opportunity to go back for his pipe, and which demonstrated in itself what a superb feat of airmanship the ditching was. Bomber Command sent congratulations 'on a very successful and gallant action', and Basil Robinson received a DSO for his part in the operation.

He had been appointed CO of 35 Squadron, posted in from 78 Squadron, since July 1941, and was hugely popular with his men. He seems to have been credited with a number of astonishing exploits. In an operation over the Alps on 18 November 1942, Robinson ordered his crews to bale out, and they did, but just as he was preparing to exit himself the flames died away, and so he flew the Halifax II home single-handed. The squadron, 35, was then in its Pathfinder period, based at Graveley. Robinson himself finally went the way of all his friends, and did not return from the first night of the air battle of Berlin, 23/24 August 1943, when he flew as a second pilot in a crew from 35 Squadron.

Early in the next year, 1942, change was in the air for Bomber Command. At Driffield the main body of 104 Squadron had left for Malta, so the home echelon of 104 was reformed as a new squadron, 158. They continued to operate with Wellington Mark IIs until they converted to Halifaxes in June 1942.

Meanwhile more Yorkshire airfields were continuing to be built apace, with the expansion of Bomber Command and of 4 Group itself. Pocklington, Dalton, Burn, Elvington, East Moor and Melbourne were all 4 Group airfields opened from 1941 onwards. Middleton St George (just over the Durham border but Yorkshire by 'adoption' because the nearest town for a night out was Darlington, with its celebrated hostelry, the Fleece), was another such 4 Group airfield opened at this time, together with its satellite of Croft, also just in County Durham but so near the border it cries out for adoption. The well known and active air stations of Snaith and Breighton near Selby, and Holme-on-Spalding Moor remained in 1 Group with their HQ at Bawtrey Hall until mid-1943, when they joined 4 Group. Alone of Yorkshire stations, Lindholme in South Yorkshire was in 5 Group, flying Hampdens from 1941 until mid-1942 and thereafter housing the Polish squadrons, Nos 304 and 305.

This coming and going and changing of squadron locations in 4 Group was also reflected in mistakes made in postings. Charlie Chapman, who ended the war as a Warrant Officer, DFM, found himself early in 1943 posted to Linton-on-Ouse and 76 Squadron, despite the fact that his flight engineer's training had been on Lancasters, and not the Halifaxes with which 76 Squadron was equipped. W/C Leonard Cheshire arranged for Charlie to be posted to a squadron operating Lancasters. At a leap, therefore, Charlie found himself in Pathfinders and 156 Squadron, with whom he concluded a highly successful and eventful tour.

Chapter 4

New Leader, New Policies

'I want you to look at the man on either side of you. In six months' time only one in three will be left, but if you are the lucky one I promise you this. You will be two ranks higher'... The Poles started to cheer.

Words of Arthur Harris from Henry Probert,
'Bomber Harris, His Life and Times'

On 22 February 1942, Air Marshal Arthur T. Harris became Commander in Chief, Bomber Command. Because of the controversy that surrounds his leadership of Bomber Command, it must be emphasized that Harris did not initiate the policy of area bombing. On 14 February 1942, a week before his appointment, a directive from Bomber Command had called for an 'offensive on a heavy scale ... (to) enhearten and encourage the Russians', and repeated the words of the directive of 9 July 1941: 'The primary objective of

---

Air Marshal Arthur T. Harris (later Air Chief Marshal Sir Arthur Harris), Air Officer Commander-in-Chief Bomber Command at work in his office at Command Headquarters, High Wycombe. With him is Air Vice-Marshal R. Saundby (later Deputy AOC-in-C). (via Graham Smith)

your operations should be focused on the morale of the enemy civil population, and, in particular, of the industrial workers.'

And so, months before Arthur Harris's appointment there had been official authorisation for the RAF to attack the centres of towns and cities. Area bombing had arrived. It had become official Air Ministry policy after the RAF's failure to hit specific targets and after daylight flights, on all but very special occasions, had been prohibited because of high casualties. Of course it was what the RAF had been created as an independent force for. The day after the February directive the Chief of Air Staff, Sir Charles Portal, clarified still further its words: 'The aiming points are to be the built up areas,' he ruled, 'not for instance, the dockyards or aircraft factories.'

Arthur Harris took over Bomber Command at a critical moment. Other Service representatives had looked forward to its dismemberment. German night defences, moreover, had been developed and extended. The so-called Kammhuber Line (after its architect, General Joseph Kammhuber) created a grid of offensive 'boxes' from Denmark to the Swiss border, each box the province of a particular Luftwaffe night fighter, orbiting a radio beacon and acting on broadcast instructions.

Electronic aids, therefore, were high on Arthur Harris's list of priorities. In a raid against Cologne on 13 March 1942, Gee ('Ground Electronic Engineering') was used for the first time, enabling a navigator to guide the aircraft to the target. Gee was a device for fixing your position other than by the fragile identification of landmarks and astro-navigation. A Gee box was installed in the aircraft, which received radio pulses transmitted from three ground stations based in England. Thus was your position established. Because of the curvature of the earth the range of Gee was 400 miles, so the Ruhr and the northern German ports were within range. For more distant targets Gee would not take you there, but would see you all right for the early part of your route. It would, however, only be a short time before German countermeasures would succeed in jamming Gee; an initial attempt occurred on 4 August 1942.

An outstandingly successful Gee trial was held on the night of 3/4 March 1942 in a raid on the Renault factory at Billancourt near Paris, with 235 aircraft participating including 59 from 4 Group. This was the largest number of aircraft despatched to one single target so far. S/L Thompson of 10 Squadron reported seeing his two 4,000 lb bombs burst right on the target, while S/L Lane of 158 Squadron saw many fires burning in the target area.

By now 150 aircraft were fitted with Gee, and a new bombing technique, 'Shaker', was devised. The bomber force was divided into three groups: illuminators, target markers and followers. Illuminators equipped with Gee would be first over the target, dropping bundles of flares at ten-second intervals, and would then back these up with high explosives. Thus the target markers would be guided to the scene, who would drop incendiaries, and the followers their high explosive.

The first 'Shaker' raid was by 211 aircraft on the Krupps works in Essen on the night of 8/9 March 1942. Even with the use of Gee, accurate bombing was frustrated by the thick industrial haze. Gee got the aircraft to the target, it could not do any more. A second Gee-guided raid on Essen mounted the next night, 9/10 March, was equally disappointing. Two aircraft from 4 Group were brought down with a loss of twelve aircrew. A 35 Squadron Halifax from Linton-on-Ouse, piloted by F/S Ganly, crashed into the sea 30 miles from Mablethorpe, and there was only one survivor from the 158 Squadron aircraft of F/L Duff, DFC, which crashed on return to the airfield. A young member of the rescue services, Cpl W.J. Hughes, entered the rear turret with an axe and hacked at the burning aluminium so that the rear gunner could escape. His bravery was recognized by an entry in the Notable War Services Despatch. F/L Duff, a South African, and his Australian co-pilot, Sgt C.A. Cornwell, RAAF, are both buried at Driffield cemetery. Years later my mother met his sister in the cemetery quite by chance when the sister was over for a visit, and, as a result of this, placed a posy on F/L Duff's grave on the occasion of his birthday every year until ill health finally prevented it.

Better results were obtained from the fourth Gee-led raid, on Cologne on the night of 13/14 March 1942. Fifty aircraft equipped with Gee marked the target accurately and almost half of the 135 aircraft following dropped bombs within five miles of the area marked with incendiaries. However, it was a bad night for 4 Group. Attempting to land at Leeming, a Whitley of 77 Squadron returning from an operation to Boulogne that took place the same night as the Cologne raid, stalled and crashed just to the north of the airfield, with the death of the entire crew. Two 78 Squadron Whitleys from Croft were also lost that night. One, piloted by Sgt McColl, a tough highlander from

Ross and Cromarty, possibly came down into the sea. The second Whitley, captained by P/O Ferris, was making its fifth attempt to land and crashed in the process. Three out of the five crew members were killed outright, and another, Sgt Davies, died subsequently from his injuries.

After the loss of these two aircraft there were no more Whitleys reported missing by 78 Squadron. It had been a gruelling war so far for them, with 55 Whitleys missing on operations since July 1940, and two more lost in training accidents.

Arthur Harris pondered how he could give the crews the necessary measure of confidence which they needed at this moment. On 28/29 March 1942, Palm Sunday, he sent 234 bombers to Lübeck on the Baltic, with much of the town destroyed by two waves of aircraft carrying incendiaries and high explosives. This was the first major success for Bomber Command against a German target. Though beyond the range of Gee, the device still helped with preliminary navigation to the target. Twelve aircraft were lost and one of the missing crews was from a 305 Squadron Wellington from Lindholme, piloted by Sgt F. Wasinski, shot down by flak while flying at 4,000 ft. All the crew became prisoners of war, and F/O Pawluk was one of the Allied officers in the 'Great Escape' from Sagan in March 1944, only to be handed over to the Gestapo and murdered.

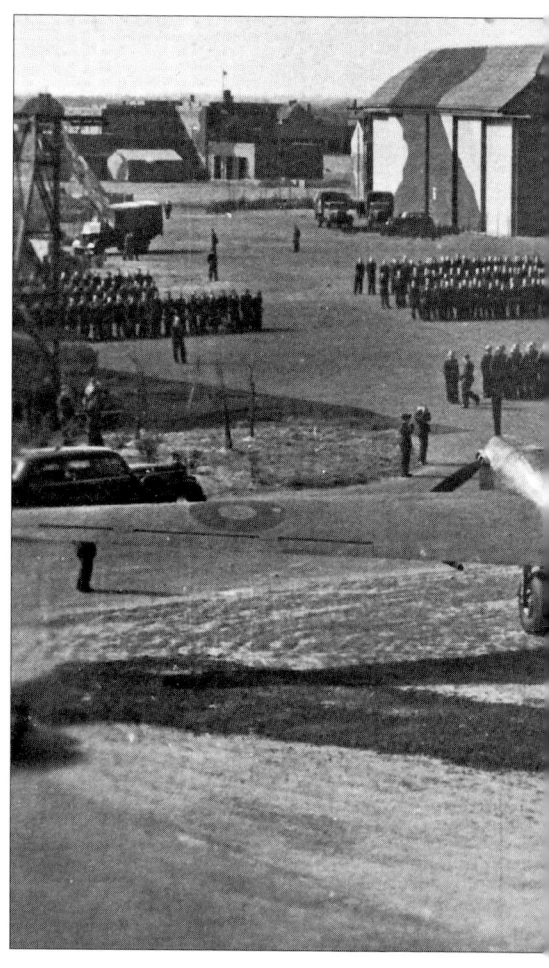

The Poles were an enthusiastic and occasionally explosive element in Bomber Command aircrew. They believed in doing absolutely all they could to outwit and defeat the enemy. They hardly ever, unless a strict order was given, brought their bombs back.

At the end of April 1942 the weather improved sufficiently for 4 Group to make an assault on the battleship *Tirpitz*, which was berthed at the Norwegian port of Trondheim and menacing Allied convoys to Russia. Merely because of its presence, the merchant ships needed an

A Wellington II of 305 (Polish) Squadron at Lindholme, spring 1942. (Peter Green)

405 Squadron – boarding their Wellington Mark IIs for their first 'op' from Driffield, in April 1941. (405 Squadron records)

unusually large number of escort vessels. Thirty-two Halifaxes from 10, 35 and 76 squadrons flew to Lossiemouth, their forward base in Scotland. Cloud and severe icing frustrated one attack, while on the night of 30/31 March out of a force of 33 Halifaxes from 4 Group, five were shot down, and only one Halifax was able to identify the target.

The *Tirpitz* attack was a classically hazardous one, with the enemy, in equal proportions, being the weather and the Germans. The *Tirpitz* was in Asen Fjord near Trondheim, and the football-shaped mines cum depth charges had to be released at a precise point, so that they could roll down underneath the ship to exploit the vulnerability of one part of the ship's hull.

On 27/28 April weather conditions again seemed to be promising and a Norwegian weather expert, specially called in, had confirmed things. Thirty-two Halifaxes from advanced bases in Scotland began the next attempt on the *Tirpitz*. As in the previous raid, Halifaxes from 10 and 35 squadrons were to attack the ship with the special mines, while aircraft from 76 Squadron, together with a group of Lancasters from 5 Group, were to tackle the defences.

This attack was one relished by W/C Don Bennett, CO of 10 Squadron and one of the Halifax pilots. It depended on key navigational ability across very few ground features at the very edge of the aircraft's range.

Over the target there was a smoke screen. Bennett was hit, and he did not release his mines. He began another run in, even though the starboard wing was burning fiercely. This time the five 1,000 lb mines were released, and Bennett had to pull up the stick to avoid the mountains between the fjord and the frontier with Sweden. He fought desperately with the controls to allow all the crew to jump. At risk to his own life, the flight engineer, F/S Colgan, came back before jumping, found the captain's parachute in the fuselage and clipped it on him. So Don Bennett was able to make his escape, jumping dangerously close to the ground, just as the starboard wing broke away.

Even so, Don Bennett's evasion was hardly straightforward. Landing in the snow, he buried his parachute and made towards Sweden. Joining up with his Wireless Operator, Sgt Forbes, the two men eventually came upon a small house, after travelling for most of the next day and existing on the Horlicks tablets and barley sugars of their escape kits. The householder showed a proper scepticism about the identity of the

two airmen, such was the fear of Gestapo *provocateurs*. Eventually they were put in touch with members of the Resistance, who took them over the border into neutral Sweden.

At an internment camp, Don Bennett and other members of the crew were officially placed under arrest. Here he and the wireless operator met up with the second pilot and flight engineer. Later they were to learn that the remaining three members of the crew had survived to become POWs. The Swedish army captain who had formally arrested them, Captain Skoogh, sent a cable, in his own name, to Bennett's wife with the single word 'Love' on it (a prearranged signal between the couple). Wartime regulations dictated that he sign it himself. Mrs Bennett, on receipt of the cable, immediately realised its significance, as she told me years afterwards. Back at Leeming the Station Commander and other senior personnel identified in the atlas the small town of Storlien in Sweden from which the cable had been sent.

After negotiation between the Swedish authorities and the British Embassy, Don Bennett was repatriated and returned to his command of 10 Squadron. It had been five weeks since he baled out over Norway. Don Bennett received a well deserved DSO, and in August of the same year took on a new role, as Commander of the Pathfinders. Eventually, he became the youngest Air Vice Marshal in the RAF.

Bennett was the founder of the Pathfinder Force (PFF) that would be so important to night bombing in the following years. Pathfinders, flying Lancasters or Mosquitoes, found the way to the target and accurately marked it with slow burning, incandescent flares for the guidance of the main bombing force. He also founded the Light Night Striking Force, using fast-moving de Havilland Mosquitos, which worked with the PFF.

Another Halifax on that raid on the *Tirpitz* in 1942, from 35 Squadron, and piloted by Canadian F/O Don McIntyre, force-landed on the frozen Lake Hoklingen. All but one of the crew, who was wounded and taken prisoner, escaped to Sweden and soon made it back to this country. The Halifax eventually sank into the icy waters, to be raised years later in June 1973 by an RAF recovery team. Today 'S for Sugar' is on display at the RAF Museum, Hendon.

It was time to turn away from the lethal business of attempting to bomb the *Tirpitz*. Air Marshal Harris was planning the '1,000 bomber' raids. Now the new Commander in Chief could demonstrate the

F/S Larry Carr, with two of those who assisted in his evasion, at risk to their own lives. (Graham Pitchfork)

potency and effectiveness of the total bomber force. And yet his front line strength was only 400 aircraft. He would need to resort to aircraft used in the Operational Training Units, flown by crews and instructors still in the training process.

Not long before the first '1,000' raid on Cologne, a remarkable story of evasion and escape occurred. F/L Larry Carr was a member of 102 Squadron flying from Dalton, whose Halifax was shot down over Belgium during a raid on Cologne on the night of 27/28 April 1942. On parachuting from the stricken Halifax he found himself in

the hands of a well organized escape organization. He was hidden on a nearby farm, given clothing, taken to a Brussels suburb by train where an identity card was produced, and handed over to a young girl who arranged to take him to Spain via Paris. He had a number of lucky escapes on the way and the two surviving members of his crew were captured. The young girl Dédée, or Andrée de Jongh, who helped him was the famous inspiration behind the Comet Line which took over 200 evading airmen across the Pyrenees to safety.

Dédée left Larry Carr at San Sebastian on the Spanish side of the Franco-Spanish border, and he was taken to the British Consul in Bilbao and then to Gibraltar and the aircraft-carrier HMS *Argus*, which brought him back to the UK. His evasion and escape is an inspiring story, not least because those who helped British airmen paid a heavy price. In the Comet Line 23 were shot, including the gendarme who had played an important role in the early stages of Carr's evasion, and Dédée's own father; 130 people were sent to Ravensbruck concentration camp and did not return, and Dédée herself spent two years in Ravensbruck. She was a truly remarkable person, who was awarded the George Medal after the war by King George VI. After recovering from a severe illness, contracted in the camp, she became a nursing sister in a leper colony in the Congo. The King of Belgium made her a countess.

Operation Millennium, the first '1,000 bomber' raid, took place on the night of 30/31 May 1942, and the target was Cologne; 41 aircraft failed to return, six from Yorkshire bases. One hundred and thirty Halifaxes took part, twelve being from 1652 Conversion Unit at Marston Moor, near York, which was commanded by Leonard Cheshire.

The second '1,000 bomber' raid was mounted the very next night when 956 bombers were sent out on 1/2 June 1942 against Essen. Thirty-six aircraft failed to return, including 15 from 4 Group and one Wellington from Lindholme, a Yorkshire base (with 305 Polish Squadron) formerly of 5 Group but now in 1 Group. The pilot, W/C Hirszbandt, OBE, DFC, had flown as a test pilot at Farnborough.

Leeming lost three of its Halifaxes and crews on this raid, Dalton lost three Halifaxes of 102 Squadron, while Breighton and 460 RAAF Squadron lost four Wellingtons. Nos 102 and 460 Squadrons would continue to be plagued by heavy losses until the end of the war.

A last '1,000 bomber' raid was mounted on the night of 25 June 1942 on Bremen. Forty-eight aircraft failed to return, including six

Halifax II of 35 Squadron, Linton-upon-Ouse in July 1942. The next month,
35 Squadron went to the PFF and moved to Graveley. (Peter Green)

Halifaxes, four of them from 102 Squadron (by now flying from Topcliffe). Yet another Wellington II from the Polish 305 Squadron at Lindholme ditched while returning to base. All the crew but G/C Skarzynski, who was Station Commander at Lindholme, and who had achieved fame for his pioneering flights pre-war, were rescued.

August 1942 saw the creation of the Pathfinder Force (PFF) under the command of W/C Don Bennett. Pathfinder methods, or rather rudimentary target-marking methods, had been used now and again for quite a while now. The Commander in Chief, Arthur Harris, vigorously argued against creating a *corps d'élite*, as opposed to having special marker crews in each squadron, but he was overruled by the Chief of Air Staff and the War Cabinet. And so by 16 August five squadrons, drawn from every bomber group, were in place on the airfields, ready to operate.

From 4 Group came 35 Squadron with its Halifaxes, who transferred from Linton-on-Ouse to the very different surroundings of Graveley, near Huntingdon. In time, by war's end, the Pathfinder squadrons numbered 19, including the Light Night Striking Force, while all squadrons not equipped with Mosquitoes were equipped with Lancasters.

On many occasions in the later part of the war, a Master Bomber directed the operations, a job which did not offer good life insurance prospects. One of 4 Group's former luminaries, Johnny Fauquier of 405 Squadron at Pocklington, was a proven Master Bomber, mixing direction with commentary and typical North American invective. He

Air Vice Marshal Don Bennett (centre) and G/C Ray Collings, Station Commander of Warboys (left of Her Majesty) escort King George VI and Queen Elizabeth during their visit to Warboys, 10 February 1944. (Ray Collings used to be CO of 35 Squadron and Don Bennett CO of 10 Squadron, both in Yorkshire). (via Taff Jones)

ultimately would have the distinction of commanding 405 (Vancouver) Squadron after it had moved to join Pathfinders and was stationed at Gransden Lodge.

A number of gifted individuals also made the transition from the Yorkshire squadrons to Pathfinders. Don Bennett took with him as a part of his staff the experienced and impressively capable F/L Angus Buchan, DFC, who had been with him on 10 Squadron as Squadron Navigation Officer. At Pathfinder HQ, Buchan was Pathfinder Force Navigation Staff Officer. Required to fly every so often, to keep in touch with contemporary developments in the air war, he lost his life a few weeks after the formation of Pathfinder Force on the night of 24/25 August 1942 in an aircraft of 83 Squadron raiding Frankfurt. Ray Silver, the navigator of a 10 Squadron Halifax which was shot down on the first '1,000' raid, and who became a POW, speaks in fulsome tones of Angus Buchan's superb encouragement of fledgling navigators on 10 Squadron at Leeming. But then he was a gifted teacher and communicator, as befitted a lecturer in Mathematics at Edinburgh University.

Chapter 5

'All Sorts and Conditions'

Dressing for the raid in the locker room had its own ritual significance, as the men climbed into their long underwear, their white operational sweaters, as the gunners fastened on their heated suits, and all zipped on their fleece-lined flying boots. Crews had their own private jokes.

Michael P. Wadsworth: 'They Led the Way'

From the very start of the war Bomber Command crews were cosmopolitan in composition. Early crews would boast of the odd Canadian or New Zealander or Australian who had sailed round the world to volunteer for the RAF. The spirit of adventure was strong for air-minded youths. Quite soon there were Royal Australian Air Force (RAAF) squadrons – 460 at Breighton in 1 Group from January 1942, 466 at Driffield and then Leconfield from late 1942, and 467 Squadron in 5 Group at Scampton, also from late 1942.

Throughout late 1942 Canadian airmen were also gathering in their squadrons on airfields north of York that eventually became accredited to the entirely new No 6 Canadian Group, Bomber Command. Temporary space was found at Linton-on-Ouse for 6 Group HQ; but by 1 December the HQ moved to Allerton Park near Knaresborough, known, especially to Canadian aircrew, as 'Castle Dismal'.

On 1 January 1943, No 6 RCAF Bomber Group officially assumed operational status. During the next three days six stations were handed over by the RAF to the Royal Canadian Air Force, with RCAF squadrons already occupying them: Leeming (with 408 and 405 squadrons, although 405 was ultimately to move to Pathfinders), Middleton St George (419 and 420 Squadrons), Dishforth (425 and 426 squadrons), Croft (427 Squadron), Dalton (428 Squadron), and last of all Skipton-on-Swale, which was still in the process of construction.

By March 1943, 6 Group included Topcliffe, housing 405 Squadron just before its migration to Pathfinders. Leeming had 408 Squadron with their Halifaxes, Middleton St George had 419 and 420 squadrons operating Halifaxes and Wellingtons respectively, Dishforth flew the Wellingtons of 425 and 426 squadrons, Croft had its 427 Halifaxes recently converted from Wellingtons, and Dalton had 422 Squadron (still with Wellingtons, yet to embark upon conversion to Halifaxes in June 1943). By the end of the war, April 1945, 6 Group's principal aircraft had become the Lancaster, mixed with Halifaxes powered with Hercules engines (a successful and well liked variant).

Linton-on-Ouse airfield became a member of 6 Group in summer 1943, when 76 and 78 squadrons moved from there to Holme-on-Spalding Moor and Breighton respectively, which became members of 4 Group. They were succeeded at Linton by 426 Squadron, which arrived from Dishforth, and conversion to Lancaster IIs was soon underway. Soon 408 Squadron moved to Linton from Leeming, to join 426, beginning immediately its Lancaster conversion programme.

Airfields in 6 Group by war's ending included, in addition, East Moor (432 Squadron with Halifaxes), Skipton-on-Swale (424 Squadron with Lancasters and 433 with Halifaxes and Lancasters) and Tholthorpe (420 Squadron with Halifaxes and Lancasters).

The operational squadrons of 6 Group gave themselves appropriate names derived from Canadian fauna or their circumstances of origin. No 408 Squadron's badge was a flying Canada goose, a powerful bird that covers vast distances, while 419 'Moose' Squadron acquired this name from its first CO, W/C John 'Moose' Fulton, DSO, DFC, AFC. The moose traditionally is a ferocious fighter, and the squadron's motto was in the Cree language. No 420 was 'Snowy Owl' Squadron, because the snowy owl is indigenous to Canada and hunts by night. No 425 was 'Alouette' Squadron, referring to the sky lark, the subject of the

Crew outside a Wellington X of 427 Squadron, Croft. (Peter Green)

French Canadian folk song, and the motto *Je te plumerai* ('I shall pluck you out of the skies') is an excerpt from the same folk song. More sinisterly, 422 was 'Ghost' Squadron with its badge a death's head in a shroud. The nickname 'Ghost' came from hours of night bombing, an activity performed at a time when only ghosts are about, a little piece of Canadian gothic in this highly technical air war.

No 429 was 'Bison' Squadron, a fierce opponent among Canadian animals. And then there was 431 'Iroquois' Squadron, with an Iroquois Indian motto, and an Iroquois warrior's head on the badge. No 434 'Bluenose' Squadron was a name derived from the common nickname for Nova Scotians, the badge depicting the famous schooner *Bluenose*, a fast and graceful ship from a bygone era. And there were 415 'Swordfish' Squadron, 424 'Tiger' Squadron, 426 'Thunderbird' Squadron, 427 'Lion' Squadron, 432 'Leaside' Squadron, and 433

71

'Porcupine' Squadron, a roll call of names and associations which brought more than a breath of Canada with them.

And yet whether aircrew aspirants were Canadians or Australians or from Britain, all would meet up and be sorted into their constituent crews at the Operational Training Units (OTUs) in this country. There were over 90 of them, and now they converted the men onto the type of aircraft they would fly and welded them together into a crew. This momentous stage in their processing and training was left to individuals. They were gathered into hangars and invited to sort themselves out into crews, a strange marriage of mixed nationalities and backgrounds.

They had reached the OTUs after volunteering for aircrew and being sent to their Initial Training Wings. As a result of success at the ITWs (and candidates fell by the wayside all the time), would-be pilots, navigators and bomb aimers were sent by the Empire Air Training Scheme to Service Flying Training Schools (SFTS) overseas in the Dominions – to Canada, mostly, but also to Australia, South Africa or Southern Rhodesia. Others went for the next stage of their training to equivalent agencies in this country. Flight engineers especially had a rigorous course at 4 School of Technical Training at St Athan in South Wales.

By whatever diverse routes, in this country or overseas, all ended up at the OTUs or the Heavy Conversion Units. Fatal accidents, due to a combination of inexperienced aircrew and worn out, overused aircraft, were high at OTUs. Nearby cemeteries tell the story of men whose operational career ended here, before it had really begun. Stonefall cemetery in Harrogate, if you should visit it, is a memorial to lost 6 Group aircrew, all those Canadian boys from Winnipeg, Toronto, Saskatchewan and the Great Lakes, who poured out their lives in the struggle for freedom a long, long way from their homes and families, before they had flown a single operation against the enemy. For a two-year training to end this way was almost unbelievable, but it often happened.

The dominance of Canadian nationals in 6 Group crews was obvious. Nevertheless there were a number of British nationals who made it onto these Canadian crews, and who were welcomed. Flight engineers, until much later in the war, tended to be from the UK, until Canadian-trained FEs started to come on-stream. And the mixture of nationalities and backgrounds led to the creation of enduring bonds. There was one crew flying in early 1944 from Leconfield on 640 Squadron (an offshoot of 158 Squadron) captained by an American, 'Doss' Kornegay, who had come to the RAF and Bomber Command via the RCAF, and his crew included two Canadians, two Scotsmen, a Brazilian and a Londoner. I met some of this crew in recent years at the Lincolnshire Aviation Museum at East Kirkby. They flew their early operations with 4 Group at Leconfield, but ended the war flying with the Pathfinders, a not uncommon experience for successful and integrated crews on the Yorkshire squadrons. Indeed it was the very variety of the crew, fostering strong ties, that welded them into an effective fighting force. As for their differences in nationality – *vive la différence.*

Holme-on-Spalding Moor, which in mid-1943 became the operational home of 76 Squadron, had a little knot of Norwegian aircrew. Three of them named Giortz, Lindaas and Bjerke were called Pip, Squeak and Wilfred, after the cartoon characters. In difficulties returning from a raid on Frankfurt, Lindaas preferred to stay at the controls after all the crew had jumped, and died when the plane crashed. After all, his brother had already been murdered by the Gestapo and he knew he was a marked man, if taken alive.

By June 1944 Elvington, near York, was occupied by two Free French Air Force squadrons of Halifaxes, entirely French in composition – 346 and 347. The French writer Jules Roy, who wrote movingly about the war in Indo-China in the 1950s, described his experiences at Elvington in his book *Return from Hell.* He also wrote two novels *The Navigator* and *The Happy Valley.*

Don't forget, too, that on Yorkshire soil but in 1 Group, two Polish squadrons, 304 and 305, flew their bomber operations from Lindholme. There were also three RAAF squadrons based in Yorkshire, flying an enormous number of sorties and sustaining, sadly, reciprocal heavy losses. They were 460 RAAF Squadron, flying from Breighton, near Selby, when it was still in 1 Group from January 1942 to May 1943, and the two RAAF squadrons based at Driffield, 462 and 466, the latter from mid 1944 until the end of the war. Their dark blue uniforms and easy approach caused many hearts to flutter in this little market town that had known so many squadrons come and go.

Whatever your nationality, what was it like when ops were on at a 4 or 6 Group bomber airfield in Yorkshire? Imagine this is at the winter end of the year. Flight commanders would report to the squadron CO the availability of aircraft and of crew, e.g. was anyone not available due to sickness? At that stage no one would know whether ops were on or not.

As soon as Group HQ received the signal from Bomber Command HQ at High Wycombe, a set timetable was activated. Round about 10.30 am a list would go up in the flight crew rooms detailing who was on the raid that night, in which crews and flying in which aircraft. It might take a while to get to that point, as serviceability, etc., of aircraft would need to be checked with ground crew chiefs. Later in the morning would come the NFT, the Night Flying Test, when crews would take up the aircraft for 40 minutes or so, with each crew member going through their set routines. Flight engineers would look at the gauges governing fuel consumption and check the servicing schedule and the fuel load. The bomb aimer would look at the bomb sight, the navigator his kit, the Gee box, and any other piece of special equipment, the gunners would fire off bursts to test the Browning machine guns, having checked that the perspex of both turrets was crystal clear and free of ambiguous blemishes.

Aussie aircrew at Breighton of 460 Squadron in April 1942. (460 Squadron records)

Bombing up a Wellington. (Graham Pitchfork)

Anything found on the NFT needing attention would have to be checked by the ground crew. They really were the unsung heroes, working in all weathers to get their aircraft (they thought it belonged to them) ready for the raid. In some instances they may have worked on the aircraft all night.

In the afternoon, there might well be two briefings, spaced out, a pre-briefing for pilots and navigators, and then a main briefing. Meanwhile aircraft were being prepared, fuel poured in, belts of snake-like ammunition being slotted along the feeder tracks into the Brownings. By this time, when the petrol bowsers came to fill up the aircraft, old hands could tell from the extent of the fuel load whether it was a short or long-distance target. Trolleys of bombs, perhaps driven by WAAFs, would be brought up to the aircraft for the attention of the armourers, waiting there beside the aircraft's bomb doors.

A main briefing at 1600 hours would put the operational meal, bacon and eggs usually, at, say 1730, and a take-off time at 2030 hours, generous spaces of time between the fixed points, but unhappily these pools of time aggravated the waiting. There was always the waiting.

51 Squadron crew outside a Halifax III designated 'Winsome Waaf'.
(51 Squadron archive)

At main briefing the CO would give orders for the doors to be locked and for the cover to be taken down from the high wall map, with a strip of ribbon marking the journey out and the journey back. Details like the timing of the Pathfinder markers would be given to the crew, the attack waves of the main force in which the crew flew, and with a time on-target for each wave. Navigation leader, bombing leader, signals leader, intelligence officer would all have their say after the CO's contribution, and questions were invited. Finally the CO would wish the crew 'Good Luck' and the men would walk out to have their meal and get ready.

Dressing for the raid in the locker room and crew room was almost ritualised. The same forced jokes, the lucky mascot that gunner's sister from Ontario had sent him, and made him promise to take on every trip. And then there were the gramophone records played in the crew room prior to departure, the slightly inappropriate, you might think, *I don't want to set the world on fire*, or *The Shrine of St Cecilia*, by the Andrews Sisters. At one station, on the afternoon before a raid this last record had been found broken. A member of the squadron was therefore hurriedly sent into York to buy a copy. It had become a powerful talisman, and this highly technical war of machinery made not one ha'p'orth of difference to the hopes and fears, prejudices and superstitions of the aircrew. After all, everyone going on the raid was, in aircrew parlance, 'dicing' that night.

The men looked like the contemporary advertisements for Michelin men in all their bulky protective clothing, almost waddling to the Bedford transport taking them to their aircraft out on the dispersals.

The ground crew, when the transport reached the aircraft, were still putting the finishing touches to the aircraft for the night. The crew chief would give the pilot the Form 700 to sign (the serviceability log),

Exhausted pilot at Pocklington after a raid, 405 (Vancouver) Squadron.
(405 Squadron records)

77

with the feeling and the understanding, 'There's nothing wrong with this aircraft. We've worked hard to prepare it for you. Now it's yours. Please, God willing, bring it back safely.'

After a quick cigarette, the ground crew, on a pre-arranged signal would plug in the 'trolley acc' (the trolley accumulator, the battery cart), and the engines would roar into life. Then the aircraft would wait their turn on the perimeter track, and after the 'green' from the Aldis lamp, would be away, with a little knot of well wishers, WAAFs and ground personnel waving them off by the control caravan.

Then came the deep period of waiting before the aircraft returned. This was the hard part, particularly for the WAAF who had driven a crew out. Ground crew waited out on the dispersals for their aircraft to come in, as the little heap of discarded cigarette ends built up, and it became obvious to them that the missing aircraft had not enough fuel to keep in the air.

And then there began another routine. When an aircraft and crew had gone missing Service Police and the Padre, the 'Committee of Adjustment' packed up their belongings, removing any questionable material and sending the effects to the next of kin. One heavily losing air station in 6 Group was Middleton St George, yet another was East Moor. A pilot at East Moor, John McQuiston, on 415 Squadron was shown a big warehouse with rows and rows of uniforms of the missing, waiting to be parcelled up and sent away. It was not a good thing, he reflected, to see that warehouse with all those uniforms, hung up, having lost their owners. It seemed all too reminiscent of a dormitory of lost souls. Official telegrams were sent immediately to the next of kin and it was left to the CO to write a personal letter to them, offering, if the crew was missing and nothing had been heard from them, a modicum of hope. Perhaps the Red Cross would ultimately confirm that they, or some of them, were prisoners of war.

There were tears in the WAAF dormitories, but not for long. A kind of Bomber Command code took over and emotions were suppressed. In the next 24 or 48 hours these entire procedures of preparation for a raid and absorption of the losses might have to be played out yet again.

And yet supposing the airmen, having gone through the routine of preparing for a raid, and waiting there in the aircraft for a green light from the Aldis lamp, were suddenly given a signal that the op was 'scrubbed' (i.e. cancelled), what then? At the puncture of the tension a cheer would go up. They would live another day, after all. The men would be taken back to the living quarters and there they would change into best blue for an unexpected night out, and it would be a race to the local pubs.

W/C George Holden began his service on 35 Squadron. He was CO of 102 Squadron at Pocklington and CO of 617 Squadron. Here seen with a fellow officer's child in front of the Officers' Mess at Woodhall Spa (now the Petwood Hotel) shortly before he was killed on the night of 15/16 September 1943 in a raid on the Dortmund-Ems canal. (via Jim Shortland)

A Wellington III at East Moor, 429 Squadron, having overshot the runway.
(Peter Green)

Sometimes the liberty bus would be laid on and airmen would pile in and be taken to York or Beverley or Darlington. Betty's Bar in York was consistently popular with its spacious underground bar – now the Oak Room of Betty's Tea Rooms – and the hundreds of aircrew signatures scratched on an enormous decorative mirror are there to this day, unlike most of the signatories who have gone now. Some of them went at the height of their youthful hopes and aspirations, going out into the night which had no earthly returning.

York was a Mecca for airmen. There were the Half Moon and the Olde Starre Inne, and the De Gray rooms for dancing. When there was more time and crews were between ops, on what was called, officially, a 'stand down', little knots of airforce blue would walk the walls of York or gaze in awe at the tall ceilings of York Minster, or take in a matinee at the cinema, prior to dancing or drinking. Then they could swap news of fellow airmen on their squadrons and speculate on how they and a handful of others were the only ones left of that group of 20 who had volunteered for aircrew training some two years before.

There were other places of resort, like the pubs near the airfields. The Buck Hotel in Driffield, dubbed affectionately 'Hangar Number Six', a name still remembered to this day, was much loved by the Australians of 4 Group who were at Driffield in the latter part of the war. Like the White Swan in Bubwith, the Buck Hotel was a place for the dark blue uniforms of the RAAF. The landlord of the White Swan kept a visitors' book, which airmen of 460 Squadron from Breighton used to sign. The book now reposes in the Australian War Memorial museum at Canberra. The Green Dragon in Beverley was popular with the Australians from nearby Leconfield, as was the Alice Hawthorn for aircrew of all nationalities at Linton-on-Ouse. The Trout just outside Driffield had a reputation for procuring, with help and a nod and a wink from local farms in that period of wartime restrictions, the most wonderful meals of farm-cured ham and eggs. The landlady became famous for her aircrew suppers, as word got around.

The aircraft was not the only place where members of a squadron died in the air war. On the morning of 19 June 1943 when the Halifaxes were 'bombing up' for the night's operation, the bomb dump at Snaith blew up, due to a faulty mechanism in one of the bombs, and ten armourers and ground staff of 51 Squadron were killed. The bomb dump had to be entirely reconstructed. In the short term, that night's operation, to bomb the Schneider armaments factory at Le Creusot in France, amazingly went ahead, with replacement bombs and armourers provided by the home of 1658 Heavy Conversion Unit at Riccall. Some bombs were actually primed by the armourers on low-loader vehicles while they were being transported to Snaith.

Traffic and rail transport had ground to a halt during the emergency, which was by no means an isolated incident on the bomber stations. A funeral for the ten who died was held in Selby Abbey on 30 June 1943. The bomb dump underwent the hazardous process of clearing up, with a number of armourers and other personnel being awarded a 'Mention in Dispatches'. It seems amazing in the light of our century's near obsession with 'health and safety' that operations went on unabated while all this difficult and dangerous work was in progress.

It is true that aircrew were made up of 'all sorts and conditions'. It would not be surprising, however, if we were to find within the 100,000 men who flew with Bomber Command evidence of aircrew who distinguished themselves in other fields. There was a lot of talent residing in this body of men, educated, most of them, far above the average. This has been remarked on from time to time, though the following three who flew from Yorkshire airbases have not had their distinction spoken of in connection with their service in Bomber Command.

F/O Charles Allbery was killed flying as navigator to F/L T. Richardson in a raid on Essen on the night of 3/4 April 1943. He was a member of 78 Squadron, flying from Linton-on-Ouse. Before the war he was a Fellow of Christ's College, Cambridge and a noted Coptic scholar, whose great contribution to learning, *A Manichaean Psalm Book*, was, incidentally, co-edited with a German scholar and published in Stuttgart in 1938. But then he had a string of papers, in German, published in German academic journals. He was the model for the young scholar, Roy Calvert, in C.P. Snow's novel, *The Light and the Dark*. His loss to early Christian studies is incalculable.

Willem Jacob von Stockum was from a Dutch family domiciled in the USA. After winning a gold medal for mathematics at Trinity College Dublin, he achieved the unique distinction of solving Einstein's field equations for a rotating cylinder. His work is often revisited by contemporary applied mathematicians, and he could have continued lecturing at Maryland University or moved to work on the Manhattan Project on the development of the atomic bomb, as he was approached to do. Instead in 1941 he chose to join the RCAF, and after teaching mathematics to aspiring aircrew became a pilot himself and joined 10 Squadron in 4 Group. On the night of 9/10 June 1944, just a few days after D-Day, he was shot down by flak, one of two aircraft from his squadron to be lost while bombing the airfield at Laval, a sacrifice by a brave and immensely gifted man.

Michael Ventris flew as a navigator from Holme-on-Spalding Moor with 76 Squadron. He survived the war to become a successful architect. But it was his private interest in the ancient language of Minoan Crete, called Linear B and written in a mysterious hieroglyphic-type script, which became his consuming passion. Ventris deciphered this, and demonstrated in the process that the language was an older form of ancient Greek. He received great acclaim for this achievement, rare in one so young and not a professional academic. Sadly, he was killed in a car crash in 1956.

Another gifted individual who served on one of the Yorkshire stations of Bomber Command was Esmond Romilly, Churchill's nephew. He was a volatile and quixotic personality, who nevertheless threw in his lot with the RCAF and with Bomber Command. He had a colourful past, for all that he had a short life. Expelled from his public school, Wellington, he fought with the International Brigade in Spain, becoming one of a handful of survivors of the Battle of Boadilla. He was married to Decca Mitford, one of the daughters of Lord Redesdale. The girls went in for political extremism. Unity Mitford, her sister, was a passionate follower of Hitler but Decca espoused the exact opposite in political affiliation as Esmond was an active Communist Party member.

Esmond had an eclectic and varied career, from selling silk stockings to running a bar in Miami. Eventually he joined the RCAF and met his end as P/O Romilly on a raid to Hamburg, as a navigator in a crew from Linton-on-Ouse captained by Sgt Whewell, one of four 58 Squadron Whitley Vs that failed to return on the night of 30 November/1 December 1941.

A different kind of talent was manifested by Denholm Elliott, who was a sergeant wireless operator/air gunner with 76 Squadron, flying from Linton-on-Ouse. He was shot down on 23/24 September 1942 in a raid on U-boat pens at Flensburg, when his aircraft had to ditch in the North Sea. Elliott spent the rest of the war in Stalag Luft VIII B, at Lamsdorff in Upper Silesia. After the war he developed a flourishing

Crews at Holme-on-Spalding Moor waiting to board aircraft for Kassel, 22/23 October 1943. (76 Squadron records)

acting career that extended from the stage to films and television. He won many BAFTA awards and had 40 feature films to his credit when he died aged 70 in 1992.

There were also a number of Americans in Bomber Command at this time. They had come via the RCAF, before America joined the war. When the United States joined the Allied war effort after December 1941, many of them opted to stay with the RCAF or the RAF and finish their tour before transferring to the USAAF with its B17s and B24s. Dan Brennan, an American novelist, has chronicled the varying fortunes of Yanks in the RAF and RCAF: *Never So Young Again* was published in 1944 (with a subtitle of *A Yank with the RAF ...wine, women and 'ops'*), *Operation Sky Drop* in 1966 and *Winged Victory* in 1967.

One interesting 'Yank with the RAF' was George Harsh. He came into the RCAF and the bomber war by a strange route. He was sentenced to hard labour on a Georgia chain gang for murder, pardoned, joined the RCAF, was commissioned for coming top of his gunner course, and became Squadron Gunnery Leader for 102 Squadron at Pocklington. On the night of 5/6 October 1942, Harsh's Halifax was shot down on a raid on Aachen; the pilot, W/O Schaw, a New Zealander, had stayed at the controls to let all the crew bale out, leaving no time for him to make his escape. George Harsh became a POW and with his early experiences was ideal material to help plan the Great Escape from Stalag Luft III, which he duly did, but being a planner and not a participator, he avoided the massacre that was in store for some of the escapees. George Harsh's fascinating life and experiences are chronicled in the autobiographical *Lonesome Road*, published in 1971.

Contrast his fate with that meted out to a Maori chief, Porakuru Patapo Pohe, or Johnny Pohe, who was murdered by the Gestapo among the rest of the 50 who took part in the Great Escape from Stalag Luft III. Johnny Pohe was a minor celebrity in Bomber Command, the first Maori to bomb a target in occupied Europe. Johnny was chosen for some of the difficult jobs, as his abilities as a pilot were recognized. On 27 February 1942 he piloted one of the Whitleys dropping paratroops on Bruneval. He was a member of 51 Squadron, then at Dishforth. After a successful tour he became a flying instructor at 24 OTU at Honeybourne, although he took 'time off' from this to fly the last '1,000 bomber' raid on Bremen.

Crews at Breighton of 78 Squadron waiting to board aircraft for Berlin on raid of 30/31 August 1943. (Graham Pitchfork)

In August 1943 Johnny arrived at 1663 HCU at Rufforth, near York, for conversion to Halifaxes, and the next month came back to 51 Squadron, at Snaith this time. On 22 September his crew were all captured after having to ditch in the North Sea. For 48 hours they floated in a dinghy until they were picked up by a German torpedo boat. At Stalag Luft III Johnny established his credentials as an expert tunneller. Johnny's only concern was that his parents should be proud of him. He had left behind him a four year old brother, Kawana, to whom he was devoted and when he had taken his farewell of his family to embark at Auckland on the troopship RMMS *Aorangi,* Johnny could not bear to say his last goodbye to Kawana, as he 'was weeping like a baby'. His family were desolated by his untimely death.

So here we have two men, an American ex-convict and a Maori chief, who both arrived at Stalag Luft III via Yorkshire airfields. Both flew these dangerous operations a long way from home for the cause of freedom, from the green hills and gentle slopes of the East Yorkshire Wolds. One was taken and the other left. The circumstances of their lives provide a remarkable Odyssey, even for those journeying along the danger-haunted byways of Bomber Command in wartime.

Chapter 6

The Battle of the Ruhr

Coned over the Ruhr for 15 minutes. Aircraft hit by flak and mid-upper gunner wounded. Very narrow escape.

From Log Book of F/O Philip Wadsworth

The year 1943 was a momentous one for Bomber Command and for her leader, Sir Arthur Harris. Three major air battles took place – the Ruhr, Hamburg and Berlin, the last of which continued for the first few months of 1944. The year also saw the introduction of two significant electronic aids which, although they needed to be tested, had a level of success that permitted the Commander in Chief to proceed with his plans and launch a strike at the heart of Germany's heavy industries, concentrated as they were in the Ruhr valley – what aircrew used to call 'Happy Valley'.

In Yorkshire in 1943 too, the situation was changing all the time. The newly arrived Canadian squadrons were occupying the North Yorkshire airfields and new airfields were under construction. Lancasters were being flown from 460 RAAF Squadron at Breighton and from 101 Squadron at Holme-on-Spalding Moor, and these airfields joined 4 Group in mid-1943 and came to be occupied by 78 Squadron and 76 Squadron respectively, both having previously operated from Linton-on-Ouse.

The change from a pre-war, brick-built airfield created during the expansion period, to a Nissen-hutted, muddy wartime station was not, as you will imagine, universally popular. The move, however, was Air Ministry policy to make Commonwealth aircrew and squadrons feel welcome and comfortable – as part and parcel of this policy 460 RAAF Squadron moved from Breighton to the solid and substantial Binbrook, while 426 and ultimately 408 Squadron from 6 Group came to Linton with their Canadian personnel and set about converting to Lancasters. No 101 Squadron, who took their Lancasters from Holme to Ludford Magna in Lincolnshire, were exchanging like for like, as their new station was nicknamed 'Mudford Magna'. From June 1943 the Breighton and Holme squadrons were flying Halifaxes, as were the whole of the rest of 4 Group.

Sir Arthur Harris was anxious to test out his new electronic radio-guidance aids. For 'Oboe' to work, Pathfinder (PFF) Mosquitoes fitted with the device flew ahead of the main force. A number of these were 'marker' aircraft and were controlled by two ground stations in England, which transmitted pulses and received signals back from them. These ground stations could then work out the aircraft's exact position. Hence they were able to transmit a signal by morse, a brief series of dots followed by a dash. When the Mosquito was over the aiming point the dashes ceased and were replaced by a low musical note. At the Telecommunications Research Establishment at Worth Maltravers near Swanage, where the device was developed, one musical technician said the low note sounded like an oboe. So 'Oboe' was its name thereafter. The marker aircraft, fitted with Oboe, would drop slow-burning target indicators and light up the target for the Pathfinders, and for the oncoming main force.

'H2S', like Oboe, was an aid to navigation as well as a blind bombing device. A receiver in the ventral position underneath the aircraft received ultrasound signals from the ground, which produced a map on a cathode ray tube inside the aircraft. As time went on, a new category of aircrew emerged who could interpret the ultrasound signals on the displayed 360° arc. A good Set Operator could differentiate not only between water and land, but between the built-up areas of a town or city and the open country surrounding it.

Wellington II of 104 Squadron at Driffield being bombed up. (104 Squadron records)

H2S was not dependent upon ground transmitters as Oboe was. Limited by range and the curvature of the earth, Oboe-equipped aircraft had to fly high. The Mark IV Mosquito could fly at 30,000 ft, and so gave Oboe a range of 300 miles, which could cover the Ruhr. But the way lay open to test both of the devices, and on 3 January 1943 the first tentative trials of Oboe were made against Essen, with 109 PFF Squadron providing the Mosquito 'marker' aircraft.

Three Essen raids, and 67 Lancaster sorties, were carried out over a four-night period. From these, two aircraft were lost, one of which was from 460 RAAF Squadron at Breighton, destined to become the squadron with the highest losses in the entire battle of the Ruhr from

March to July 1943. Captained by Sgt Brooks, it had an all-Australian crew except for the flight engineer, Sgt Watson. All the crew were killed. The same fate overtook the other doomed aircraft, another Lancaster from 101 Squadron at Holme-on-Spalding Moor, captained by a New Zealander, F/S Waterhouse.

After these Oboe-assisted raids, Sir Arthur Harris was eager to begin his major Ruhr offensive. Yet another diversion was in prospect, however, and Bomber Command was ordered to bomb the Biscay ports, Lorient and Saint-Nazaire, as the Battle of the Atlantic was going badly for the Allies. If Sir Arthur Harris believed that only the RAF could win the war, it was no less true that he recognised that the Navy could lose it, especially in view of the U-boat threat to British shipping. Nonetheless he chafed at delaying the opening of the Battle of the Ruhr. The diversion took two months, eight raids being made on Lorient and a single heavy attack involving 400 aircraft on St Nazaire. The weather in January and February 1943 was appalling.

But the enemy's homeland was also receiving attention during this period. Two medium-sized raids were mounted on Berlin on successive nights (16 and 17 January). In the first of these only one 5 Group Lancaster was lost, and the report from Bomber Command mentions the lightness of the defences. The German city had not been bombed since the disastrous attack in November 1941. And so the raid was repeated the next night (17/18 January). This time the defences had sharpened up, and 19 Lancasters and three Halifaxes were missing. One of two

Halifaxes missing from 76 Squadron at Linton-on-Ouse was piloted by Capt Bjorn Naess of the Royal Norwegian Air Force. He and the navigator, his fellow countryman Lt Bjarne Indsith, were among the first Norwegians on the squadron. The celebrated broadcaster Richard Dimbleby, as a BBC War Correspondent, was granted a place in Guy Gibson's 106 Squadron's Lancaster to Berlin that night, and made a famous radio report from the aircraft.

'Gardening' operations – dropping mines over the sea – were another feature of life in the early months of 1943. One took place on the same night as the Essen raid of 9/10 January. The five Halifaxes, two Lancasters and one Wellington lost included one aircraft from 158 Squadron, then at Rufforth, brought down by flak, one from 10 Squadron at Melbourne, and the first loss from 51 Squadron since they returned to Snaith from their sorties with Coastal Command.

419 Squadron Halifax II/I early 1943 at Middleton St George (Peter Green)

Sgt Banks-Martin, pilot of the Snaith Halifax, was one of several New Zealanders then on the squadron, with an all-Canadian crew. 'Gardening' ops were deadly. Flakships usually got you and you were too low to do anything about it.

The night of 30 January saw an H2S trial against Hamburg, when 148 aircraft of 1 and 5 Groups set out. Results were inconclusive, as the aircraft battled against severe weather conditions. One squadron which steadily lost aircraft during the opening months of 1943 was 101 at Holme-on-Spalding Moor, still in 1 Group. They lost one Lancaster that night, piloted by a Canadian, F/S Campbell, which included two other Canadians and one South African, Sgt Debeurier in the crew. The flak of the Kriegsmarine in the north of Holland accounted for them.

On 4 February 1943 Sir Arthur Harris received on his desk the Casablanca Directive, a report from the Casablanca Conference, where for ten January days chiefs of staff and senior political figures amongst the Allies set out the aims and objectives in the future direction of the war. The head of the USAAF, General Eaker, received the same report, and the terms in which it was spelled out were clear and unequivocal: 'Your primary object will be the progressive destruction of the German military, industrial and economic systems and the undermining of the morale of the German people to a point where their capacity for armed resistance is fatally weakened.'

The directive went on to specify the following primary objectives of the bomber offensive in order of importance: 'German submarine construction yards; the German aircraft industry; transportation; oil plants; other targets in enemy war industry'. Berlin, meanwhile, was to be attacked 'when conditions are suitable for the attainment of specially valuable results unfavourable to the morale of the enemy or favourable to that of Russia'.

Sir Arthur Harris was developing the flexible instrument he had at his disposal – 31 heavy bomber squadrons and 13 medium bomber squadrons, 15 of them equipped with Lancasters. February 1943 saw a variety of targets at Hamburg, Cologne and Turin, while tests with H2S in the Pathfinders continued all the time.

As a response to the Casablanca Directive to destroy German submarine construction yards, a large raid was mounted on Wilhelmshaven on 11/12 February. Two squadrons that always seemed to be on the 'missing' list, 101 from Holme-on-Spalding Moor and

102 Squadron Halifax Mark III Series I (Special) taking off to bomb Le Creusot from Pocklington, 19 June 1943 – Sgt Dargavel and crew in O7743 'O for Orange'.
(Peter Green)

102 from Pocklington, lost one aircraft each. The Pocklington crew, captained by Sgt H.E. Saunders, almost made it but crashed trying to make an emergency landing near Dalton airfield in North Yorkshire. Some of the crew lie in the lovely churchyard of St Catherine's church, Barmby Moor, quite near to their home airfield, where there are many Commonwealth War Graves Commission headstones. Three further raids on Wilhelmshaven followed, the last one being on 24 February.

The Ruhr assault began at 2100 hours on the night of Friday, 5 March 1943 when a single Mosquito of 109 (PFF) Squadron dropped its red target indicators, the primary markers, on an aiming point in the middle of Essen. This aircraft and seven others of 109 Squadron were

equipped with Oboe. It was classic blind marking procedure of a most accurate kind, and the main force which followed, 407 in number with 35 Pathfinder aircraft preceding, bombed through cloud and industrial haze. It was a highly successful raid, but 14 aircraft were missing, including four from the Canadian 6 Group, their baptism of fire.

Within the week a second major raid took place on Essen, on the night of 12/13 March 1943. This caused severe damage to the Krupps munitions complex, the heaviest yet, and was another successful Oboe-led operation. The 457 aircraft that took part were an indicator of the strength of Bomber Command, but 23 were missing, 13 of them from Yorkshire-based squadrons in 4 or 6 Groups. No 102 Squadron at Pocklington lost three. Sgt Charlebois, piloting one of these, held the aircraft steady until it was too late to make his own escape; he wouldn't bale out while the navigator, Sgt Hughes, was still in the aircraft.

P/O Peter Nevines, who baled out of a 76 Squadron aircraft, had an

adventurous time in the POW camp. He made three escape attempts, and was third time lucky in October 1944. He managed to change identity with a guardsman of the Coldstreams. Eventually Nevines and his escape partner sought to meet the Russian advance in January 1945. In typical fashion they were put in gaol for a number of weeks, as our Russian allies refused to be persuaded as to their true identities. Amongst the Russians were other British 'captives'. Eventually they were all marched to Wrenschen where they met about 500 American officers, and were repatriated via Odessa, Port Said, Cairo and thence to the UK, arriving home on 18 March 1945, two years and one week since Halifax DT751 MP-C had set off on the night of 12/13 March 1943 from Linton-on-Ouse to Essen.

Amongst the raids of that hectic first month of the Ruhr air offensive were some large and significant raids on non-Ruhr targets. A successful attack on Nuremberg was made on 8/9 March 1943, which was well out of the range of Oboe but was virtually an H2S trial. All the crew baled out successfully from a 102 Squadron aircraft and two of them, the bomb aimer Sgt A.R. Manfield together with the flight engineer, Sgt Hughes, managed to evade and make their way back to England.

Two other significant non-Ruhr attacks were mounted, to Munich on 9/10 March and Stuttgart on 11/12 March, although on this last raid results were disappointing. The eight aircraft lost on the Munich raid included two from 77 Squadron at Elvington. One Halifax was piloted by S/L Sage, who served in the RAF, with a short break, until 1964. Twenty years after this he became Life President of the Yorkshire Air Museum at Elvington and devoted himself to this museum's affairs until he died on 9 May 1994.

One heavily losing squadron on the Stuttgart raid was 405, which had returned from its secondment to Coastal Command early in March and now lost four of its Halifaxes. Thirteen men from the four aircraft became POWs and a remarkable seven evaded capture. One of the evaders, rear gunner Sgt Dmytruk, RCAF, joined forces with the Maquis and was killed in combat with German forces on 9 December 1943. Inevitably this sort of thing happened more and more as evaders threw in their lot with those of the French Resistance who helped them. In a short while, 405 would join Pathfinders and move to the airfield at Gransden Lodge in Bedfordshire.

During the week of the raid on Stuttgart the RAF lost 66 bombers.

Rear turret of Halifax. (Graham Pitchfork)

On the night of 29/30 March 1943 a split attack took place on both Bochum and Berlin. Twenty-one were lost in the Berlin attack, and twelve Wellingtons failed to return from Bochum. Among the latter were two Wellingtons of 196 Squadron from Leconfield. On the Berlin raid, likewise, Yorkshire losses made themselves felt – two 428 Squadron Wellingtons from Dalton, two East Moor 429 Squadron Wellingtons, two 460 (RAAF) Squadron Lancasters from Breighton, and one from 76 Squadron at Linton-on-Ouse.

Another raid on Essen, the most successful yet, took place on the night of 3/4 April, the first in which more than 200 Lancasters had participated. Losses were again high, with two missing from Snaith and 51 Squadron and four from Linton-on-Ouse.

On the night of 4/5 April 1943 the largest raid on Kiel in the war took place, involving 577 aircraft. At Snaith airfield a 51 Squadron aircraft narrowly escaped crashing into a train on take-off. The fence at the end of the runway was next to the Selby-Doncaster railway line and part of the Edinburgh to London line. The aircraft, piloted by Sgt Claude Wilson, had a stream of dense smoke pouring from it as it came

down the runway. What had happened was that the automatic fire extinguishers had come on and dampened the ignition sparks of the four engines. The pilot forced the aircraft's tail back down and swung it to port, narrowly missing an oncoming train with 13 coaches full of service personnel. No one was hurt, and the other bombers could take off for Kiel. Disaster, utter disaster had been narrowly averted.

Two aircraft failed to return to Leeming from this raid, one from 405 Squadron and one from 408 Squadron, and two equally failed to return to Melbourne from 10 Squadron, while 460's loss of a Lancaster perpetuated their reputation as a jinx squadron. There was one aircraft missing from 51 Squadron, that piloted by F/L A. Emery, DFM, who was practically the longest surviving aircrew member, since the very start of the bombing offensive, and was thought to be indestructible.

Back to the Ruhr. Beginning on the night of 8/9 April 1943, there were three raids on Duisburg within two weeks with, again, losses for the Yorkshire squadrons. However, a classic evasion took place after a raid on Frankfurt on the night of 10/11 April. G/C John Whitley, Station Commander of Linton-on-Ouse, was a passenger in a 76 Squadron Halifax piloted by F/L Hull. Shot down by a night fighter, the pilot was killed, three of the crew were injured, and four evaded. G/C Whitley was one of these, making it back to Linton to take up his job again after 45 days.

G/C Whitley's escape was considerably assisted by the fact that he wore a suit of French cut underneath his flying clothes, and had a civilian tie rolled up inside a peaked cloth cap in a small haversack he attached to his parachute strap. He wore, of course, a service shirt, but underneath that was a blue check shirt with attached collar. All this, as well as the smaller things he carried. Escape and evasion is about detail – so Whitley carried a razor, a tube of brushless shaving cream, a toothbrush, a nail file and a small compass.

Shot down over Belgium, Whitley landed in someone's back garden, narrowly escaping spiked iron posts. The family were friendly, and he was put in touch with the underground movement. From Belgium he was moved to France and the town of Bayonne, and thence to the border town of St Jean de Luz. An exhausting walk followed, over the Pyrenees and San Sebastian. From Gibraltar he was taken by Dakota to London. On return, he resumed his job as Station Commander at Linton, though few recognized him on his first venture into the Mess.

Halifax BIII of 77 Squadron. (Peter Green)

He was awarded the DSO, his exploits being described by the Air Ministry as 'one of the classic examples of evasion the war produced'.

G/C Whitley was fully conscious of the cost to those who helped evading or escaping aircrew. Three of his helpers were executed by the Germans, another died of torture in a Gestapo prison, while another man had been so badly wounded in the legs that he walked with a pronounced limp for the rest of his life. Whitley had the difficult task of visiting everyone to thank them just after the war. Only then did he become fully aware of how many of the escape line who had spirited him out of France, infiltrated by traitors and collaborators, had perished.

A raid that took place on the night of 16/17 April 1943, together with a parallel raid on Mannheim, failed badly and cost the RAF 54 aircraft, the greatest loss rate so far. The target was Pilsen in Czechoslovakia, where the Skoda works produced thousands of tons of war material for the Reich.

Three hundred and twenty-seven aircraft went to bomb Pilsen. A large asylum a few miles from the intended target was mistaken for the

Skoda factory, and was bombed in error. The factory was unharmed, although 200 German soldiers were killed in their barracks nearby. No 408 Canadian Squadron from Leeming lost four of its Halifaxes, and 102 Squadron from Pocklington lost one, piloted by S/L Lashbrook, DFC, DFM, who, having served with 51 Squadron at Snaith, was beginning his second tour. Happily he evaded and made it back to the UK, with three other members of the crew. Two 158 Squadron aircraft were missing from the Pilsen raid. From one of these, captained by F/O Bertera, four evaded, including the pilot. Clearly evasion for members of some crews, hard and costly though it was for many reasons, was becoming increasingly an option. Large numbers of aircraft brought down could mean significant numbers of airmen on the run.

For Snaith, the Pilsen raid was their worst night yet, with five Halifaxes missing. Linton-on-Ouse and 76 Squadron had four missing, and with two missing from 78 Squadron, the station had lost six aircraft in all.

The same night, 271 aircraft bombed Mannheim. This was an effective attack, happily for Bomber Command, although 18 aircraft were missing. Breighton lost three Lancasters, including the first Lancaster III, piloted by F/S White, DFM. A Wellington from 466 Squadron at Leconfield failed to return, shot down over France. The average age of the crew, captained by F/S Tozer, RAAF, was 20.

As always during the air campaigns centred on one area of assault,

Halifax II Series I (Special) 78 Squadron at Breighton. (Peter Green)

the enemy must be kept guessing. To go for the Ruhr every time would find them prepared and waiting. Thus a low level attack was planned on Stettin in the Baltic. Out of 339 aircraft that set out on the night of 20/21 April 1943, 21 failed to return, 6.2% of the total force. In the face of recent losses this would have been unacceptable to the Command, were it not for the fact that the Stettin raid turned out to be the most successful attack beyond Oboe range in the entire Ruhr offensive, with good Pathfinder marking and a notable follow up by the main force. Large parts of the centre of Stettin were devastated and production at a number of factories came to a halt.

Meanwhile this relentless war of attrition was hitting other squadrons hard too. On the night of 26/27 April, 561 aircraft attacked Duisburg. Among the 17 missing aircraft were two from Snaith and one from Elvington, 77 Squadron – the navigator was F/O R.C. Stewart, who became a POW and took part in the mass breakout from Stalag Luft III, only to be one of the 50 murdered by the Gestapo in March 1944.

There was an Oboe-led raid on Essen on 30 April/1 May 1943, when 305 aircraft were sent out and twelve failed to return. Snaith lost its token single aircraft (a steady one or two a raid and often many more); but it was nemesis for Elvington and 77 Squadron, who lost three (19 airmen killed, and three prisoners). On the night of 4/5 May, 596 aircraft attacked Dortmund, the largest non-'1,000' bomber raid of the war so far. Not only did 31 aircraft fail to return but a further seven crashed at or near their aerodromes.

Another raid on Duisburg on 12/13 May saw Snaith and 51 Squadron lose four Halifaxes. The fourth aircraft, hit by flak and yet brought down by a night fighter, tragically fell on a local bakery on the Belgian-Dutch border, killing the owner's wife and daughter.

The largest raid in the Battle of the Ruhr occurred on the night of 23/24 May 1943 against Dortmund. It was successful, but 38 aircraft were missing. Yorkshire-based aircraft suffered grievously – three aircraft were missing from 10 Squadron at Melbourne; Linton-on-Ouse lost four (two 76 and two 78 Squadron Halifaxes); 101 Squadron (still 1 Group) lost two Lancasters from Holme-on-Spalding Moor; and Middleton St George lost two 419 Squadron Halifaxes. But this raid was the third example in an operational period of less than six months that 51 Squadron at Snaith had lost or written off five Halifaxes in one night.

During this raid on Dortmund, a Wellington of 431 Squadron, flying from Burn, would have been another casualty that night were it not for the courage and skill of the aircraft's bomb aimer Sgt Sloan.

He flew, as bomb aimer, with a pilot who had recently joined the squadron, and released the bombs from 17,000 ft.

Turning away from the target, Sloan's Wellington was 'coned' by an enormous cluster of searchlights. The classic way out of this situation was to dive the aircraft steeply, which the pilot duly did. There seemed no prospect of recovery from the Wellington's steep dive and the order to 'bale out' was given. Sgt Sloan went to collect his parachute from the nose of the aircraft. Meanwhile the pilot exited through the escape hatch. The aircraft was still diving steeply, and there were still crew aboard, who hadn't heard the pilot's command.

Sloan decided the immediate concern was to get the aircraft level and under control. Fighting the controls, he at last managed to level out the aircraft. When the navigator, Sgt Parslow, came forward, he found Sloan in the pilot's seat, sitting sideways, with his parachute on. Sloan found the aircraft was handling moderately well, although searchlights were still on it, and the Wellington was still being harassed by light flak. He did a quick check; the navigator and wireless operator were still in the aircraft. There was no reply, during this check, from the rear gunner so, Sloan thought, he too must have baled out.

Sloan took charge in the pilot's seat. He had no previous experience, but he had always shown a great interest in the pilot's job, had stood beside him in the cockpit, and had had several turns at flying the link trainer. This apparently casual interest became a life saver. First, Sgt Sloan shook off the searchlights clustering round his aircraft with remarkable corkscrewing, twists and dives. He then checked with the two other members of the crew, the navigator Sgt Parslow, and the wireless operator, F/O Bailey that they were willing to stay in the aircraft rather than bale out.

The navigator took a visual fix, and the Wellington was making for nearest landfall on the East Anglian coast. It was then that they realised the port engine was out of pitch, with a rise in its revolutions. They were now over Cottesmore in the UK, and had difficulty in keeping to a reasonable height. Once again, when Sloan checked with his two colleagues as to whether they wanted to bale out, they chose to stay. Finding an airfield close by with a simple flare path, and just as the

Halifax II Series I (Special) of 10 Squadron in flight. (Peter Green)

aircraft was becoming impossible to control any longer, Sloan lowered the undercarriage and began the approach to land. F/O Bailey fired Very signals, and the control was alerted. Avoiding the boundary fence, the engine failed. Nevertheless the intrepid Sgt Sloan made a good landing, with no more damage to the aircraft and without injury to any of the three of them.

He had landed at RAF Cranwell. To this day, it is remembered as a magnificent feat for a seasoned pilot, let alone a bomb aimer with a tentative knowledge of the pilot's trade. Sgt Sloan was given an immediate Conspicuous Gallantry Medal, which ranks just below the Victoria Cross as the highest award open to NCOs. Sgt Sloan was also commissioned in the field; he was sent on a pilot's course and in 1945 completed a successful tour with 158 Squadron at Lissett. He ended the war as a Flight Lieutenant with the DFC, and was subsequently an officer on the King's Flight. On leaving the RAF, Sloan gave a number of years' service to the ATC, commanding the Edinburgh wing and retiring as a Wing Commander in 1975.

Sgt Sloan was not the only member of the crew to be honoured on that eventful night of 23 May 1943. F/O Bailey received the DFC, and Sgt Parslow the DFM.

Bomber fleets of 700-plus bombed the cities of the Ruhr. Dortmund, already mentioned, was the biggest raid, but Bochum, Mülheim,

Gelsenkirchen, Krefeld and Wuppertal were attacked. There was another large raid of 783 aircraft on Düsseldorf on the night of 11/12 June 1943, while the same night 72 Pathfinder aircraft set out for Münster on a mass H2S trial. Snaith lost another three aircraft that night. The squadron had to renew itself three times over.

The 'bouncing bomb' Dambusters Raid the previous month, on the night of 16/17 May, had had a significant effect on the industry of the Ruhr. Less than a month later the 'Pointblank' Directive, including the final proposals emanating from the Casablanca Conference, was formally issued to Bomber Command and the USAAF. Pointblank underlined the urgent need to check the enemy's fighter strength as top priority, and highlighted the clutch of industries upon which the enemy's fighters depended.

The final raid of the Ruhr battle was on 30 July 1943 against Remscheid, with losses above the average, 15 crews out of 273 failing to return. The complete tally of this hectic time had been 40 major raids in 19 weeks, 872 aircraft lost from 18,506 sorties flown. It was remarkable that in the middle of such a hectic air battle, the like of which had not been seen before, 4 Group squadrons began to be equipped with new, improved Halifaxes, Marks II and V (Series I-Special). Mark Vs also went to the Canadian squadrons in 6 Group. And yet Handley Page and the aircraft engineers were seeking to improve the aircraft the whole time, in the middle of the ebb and flow of major offensives. Indeed by the end of 1943, all the Mark II Halifaxes in 4 Group had been replaced by the further improved Halifax Mark III.

The Ruhr offensive was over. It would be accurate to say that both Bomber Command and the German people were reeling from its effects. The Ruhr had been well nigh pulverised with the consequent disruption and dislocation of many of its heavy industries. Bomber Command had suffered severe losses but already the Commander in Chief, Bomber Command, was turning his attention towards Hamburg, Germany's second city, even before the last raid on the Ruhr was complete. For one thing, technology had made it accessible. Although it was not within Oboe range, it gave an excellent H2S picture on the cathode ray screen inside the aircraft.

The Battle of Hamburg, prepared for since a Bomber Command Directive some time in May 1943, had begun.

Chapter 7

Hamburg and Peenemünde

In a moment the mid-upper gunner yelled out, 'There's a fighter coming in. He's got a Lanc – and another – and another.' In a matter of seconds one German fighter had sent three Lancasters to earth in flames.

G/C Sam Hall in M. Wadsworth's 'They Led the Way '

Operation **'Gomorrah'** was a Bomber Command plan to destroy Hamburg, Germany's second city. The name of the operation derived from the biblical story in the book of Genesis, about the Almighty casting fire from heaven upon the cities of Sodom and Gomorrah. The RAF had already visited it 137 times but it would be a tough nut to crack, with its defences of more than 50 heavy flak guns, 166 88mm guns and 96 103mm and 128mm guns. The crisis in the Battle of the Atlantic, though eased considerably since the critical days of 1941 and early 1942, was by no means over, and Hamburg had built over one third of the U-boats on patrol in the northern oceans.

Seven hundred and ninety-one aircraft were sent out on the first Hamburg raid on 24/25 July 1943. For the first time a device was used which distorted the German radar, rendering it useless. It was called 'Window', and consisted of strips of aluminium foil, 27cm long by 2cm wide, stuck to pieces of black paper. One member of a bomber's crew pushed out the strips of Window. With so much of it in the air, fluttering down like a snowstorm, the Würzburg radar, which guided the searchlights and the flak guns, was almost put out of action. The Window strips were like bombers reproducing themselves infinitesimally on the radar screen. Furthermore the Luftwaffe night fighters could not be vectored on to the British bombers.

Thus the total bomber losses that night were light, for a major raid like this one. The usual heavily losing Yorkshire bomber squadrons lost one each – 76 Squadron, after much wandering, since the previous month settled at their permanent wartime home at Holme-on-Spalding Moor, 102 Squadron from Pocklington, 51 Squadron from Snaith, 158 Squadron from Lissett, and 460 RAAF Squadron now at Binbrook, after a move from Breighton.

The next night, 25/26 July, 705 aircraft attacked Essen, a city within Oboe range as Hamburg was not. Not to leave

Messerschmitt Me 110, with pilot Gerhard Herzog (far right) who shot down a Manchester. (Peter Green)

Hamburg alone, six Mosquitoes visited it that same night. Heavy damage was done (Window was still effective), particular devastation being inflicted on the Krupps armament factory – the next morning Dr Gustav Krupp, the owner of the factory, suffered a permanently damaging stroke, which would later save him from being arraigned for war crimes at Nuremburg. Twenty-six aircraft failed to return (the

Group of 51 Squadron principals at Snaith.
(51 Squadron archive)

Germans were learning to hit back against and despite the background of Window) and 4 Group sustained a loss of eleven aircraft.

The crew of one of the lost aircraft, a Wellington X from Skipton-on-Swale, were all rescued after ditching a mile away from the Norfolk coast. In this rescue there was a heartwarming thread of cooperation extending between the Cromer lifeboat, the landlord and his staff at the Red Lion Hotel, and the RAF station at Coltishall, who kitted out the dishevelled crew for their return to Skipton-on-Swale, where they were back within 24 hours.

The month of the Hamburg raids, July 1943, was an exceptionally dry period in northern Europe. So, when a third raid on Hamburg was planned for the night of 27/28 July, temperatures were around 30°C, even in the early evening, and humidity was at 30%. The 787 bombers sent out that night created a firestorm, a mass of fire that burst and spread and created its own raging wind that went through the workers' houses like a tinderbox. Water supplies failed. The fires could not be fought. Air was used up by the flames. People were suffocated in air raid shelters, or got caught in the all-encompassing firestorm. Some jumped into the canal to escape the fire, and were drowned. The death toll reached 40,000. British losses were 17 aircraft.

In the aftermath of this raid, over a million people left Hamburg, telling their dreadful tale wherever they came to seek refuge. The firestorm raged unchecked, until it had consumed all combustible material to hand. The ingredients of the raid that produced the firestorm were exactly the same as those used in all other previous raids on cities. What had produced this man-made disaster was not the bomb load, or a particular combination of incendiaries with high explosives, but the weather, and particularly that unusual combination of high temperature, low humidity and tinder dry conditions on the ground.

Six of the 17 missing aircraft were Yorkshire-based, four from 4 Group and two from 6 Group. A 76 Squadron aircraft from Holme-on-Spalding Moor was attacked during the firestorm raid by two Luftwaffe fighters in a typical *Wilde Sau*, 'Wild Boar', operation – a target of opportunity and single-engined aircraft working in pairs. P/O Elder ordered the four uninjured crew to bale out, on approaching the USAAF base of Shipdham in Norfolk, and made a successful crash landing.

The two 6 Group aircraft, a Halifax II from 408 Squadron at Leeming and a Wellington X from 429 Squadron at East Moor, were both shot

Halifax II Series IA of 434 Squadron at Tholthorpe. (Peter Green)

Halifax III shot down near Münster on Berlin raid of 31 August 1943, from 102 Squadron, Pocklington. The pilot Sgt. E.T.S. Rowbottom and four others in the crew were killed. One became a POW and one evaded. (Peter Green)

down by night fighters. Despite Window, excessive glow showed up the silhouettes of the aircraft and the Germans, in a proper mood of revenge, went hunting, freed from the constraints of radar prediction and guidance. The Wellington was piloted by W/C Piddington, who had only a month before been posted to command the squadron. He was killed and only two of his crew, the gunners, survived to become prisoners of war. Not long after this loss 429 Squadron moved to Leeming and began the conversion process to Halifaxes. W/C Piddington was not the only CO to be lost in action by 429 Squadron. On 22/23 June W/C Savard, DFC, had been lost over Mulheim, at 22 years old the youngest CO in Bomber Command.

A third raid on Hamburg on the night of 29/30 July 1943 by 777 aircraft was successful and large parts of Barmbek, power stations, gasworks, and a firm which designed submarines were destroyed. A wireless operator from Snaith, Sgt Hart commented, however, 'It was like heaving coals into a furnace.'

Bomber Command was paying a price, as losses, at 28 missing aircraft, were high. No 76 Squadron, as was usual, lost one Halifax V, piloted by one of that gallant little band of Norwegians who gravitated to the squadron, whose friendship and relaxed open manner were infectious but whose courage and determination were awesome. Lt Bjercke of the Royal Norwegian Air Force had only been posted to the squadron

Sir Guy Lawrence: as W/C G.K. Lawrence he was CO of 78 Squadron, Breighton from August 1943 to April 1944. (Peter Green)

just over a fortnight before. First the flak got his aircraft, and a waiting night fighter finished the job. He and his navigator perished, while five of his crew, including a fellow countryman, Sgt Olsen, RNAF, became prisoners of war.

It was just as well for Bomber Command that this third Hamburg raid was successful. For the fourth and last raid to Hamburg by 740 aircraft on the night of 2/3 August 1943 was a failure – if a set of unique weather conditions had delivered the essential requirements of the firestorm, it was another set of weather conditions that saved

Three Halifax IIs of 10 Squadron in flight. (Peter Green)

Crashed aircraft of 76 Squadron at Holme-on-Spalding Moor. (Peter Green)

Peenemünde – before and after the bombing. (Graham Pitchfork)

Hamburg. A violent thunderstorm across Germany caused 186 aircraft to turn back or to seek alternative targets. Four aircraft, due to icing, excessive turbulence or lightning strikes, simply dropped from the sky. St Elmo's fire played around guns and propellers, and compasses ceased to function. That night the weather was indeed the more powerful enemy. As they waited for the signal out on the perimeter track on their airfields, aircrew fully expected a 'scrub'. But it was not to be. They flew out in the teeth of the storm, through towering cumulo-nimbus thunder clouds.

Thirty aircraft were lost. The Pathfinders could not even mark the area they were aiming for. Bombing was, in consequence, desultory and scattered and the German fighters took a toll of crippled, disorientated machines and crews. Any Window the crews could push out was soon scattered and blown away on the storm. Würzburg radars renewed their effectiveness, as night fighters were vectored towards the British bombers. A 10 Squadron Halifax II from Melbourne, attacked by a Junkers Ju 88 and severely crippled, crash landed on return. No one was injured; the pilot, F/O Jenkins received an immediate DFC, and the Canadian rear gunner, Sgt Hurst a DFM, and was credited with shooting down the night fighter.

Within 15 days of the fourth and final raid of the battle of Hamburg the bombers, 596 of them, went to Peenemünde, a research establishment on the Baltic coast where V-weapons, the new rocket-propelled bombs, were being made and tested. The raid was a successful one, setting back the V-weapons programme by two months at least. But the price was high: 40 bombers failed to return.

Like the Dambusters raid, or the raid in June on Friedrichshafen, the Peenemünde raid on 17/18 August had a Master Bomber, or, as he was called then, a Master of Ceremonies. This was G/C John Searby, whom we first encountered in 405 Squadron at Pocklington in November 1941. John Searby had had a brilliant career in Bomber Command, and was now CO of 83 (PFF) Squadron at Wyton. He had the dangerous job of flying to and fro over the target while the attack was in progress and of keeping the whole thing together, no mean task on such a complicated raid with three individually timed waves of aircraft and three separate aiming points. When Searby arrived back at Wyton, after successfully fulfilling his perilous commission, his clothing, under his flying jacket, was soaked in perspiration.

A Halifax III lands at Breighton. (78 Squadron records)

In the preparations for the raid a high level of security was implemented, and the atmosphere of 'something important' rapidly sped through the aircrews. At 76 Squadron at Holme-on-Spalding Moor, for instance, the officer briefing told the crews that 'if you don't get it tonight, you'll have to go back tomorrow night'. The crews were not let into the secret of Peenemünde. It might be thought that that would have added a measure of red hot zeal to the enterprise, but aircrew did not usually need such an extra stimulus.

Low flying was the order of the day. Crews attacked at a height between 4,000 and 8,000 ft, and 75% of the bomb loads were made up of high explosive. It was bright moonlight, literally a good night-fighter night, when the aircraft set out. The raid, starting with the first wave, was to unfold from 0013 hours and began with red spot flares, dropped by the Pathfinders over Rügen Island. G/C Searby made seven runs over the target, while a diversionary raid on Berlin by eight Mosquitoes lured away most of the night fighters for the first part of the raid.

The losses on the raid, of 40 aircraft, were mostly suffered by those flying in the last wave: aircraft of 5 Group, who lost 17, and those of the Canadian 6 Group, who lost 13 out of 57 aircraft. By the time they were over the target some night fighters had realized the air raid on Berlin was a spoof.

So many stricken aircraft had dived into the sea. So many names to be inscribed on the Runnymede memorial. When Canadian Bill Swetman returned to Linton-on-Ouse to find that his CO, W/C Crooks had been killed, he was promoted to Wing Commander and became CO of 426 Squadron at the age of 23. It was certainly a young man's war.

Peenemünde made the crews used to a higher scale of casualties again, after the successes over Hamburg. For Sir Arthur Harris was gearing himself up to the offensive against Berlin, and though what is called the Battle of Berlin opened on 18/19 November, three attacks were mounted against the Big City in late August and early September 1943, which were an exercise in themselves of enduring heavy casualties in order to inflict heavy damage on the enemy's capital. But, as we shall see, Berlin was no Hamburg, conveniently located near the north German coast. It was, rather, a city too far.

Harvest scene at Elvington. On 4 October 1943 the aircraft in the picture, R-Roger, a Halifax II Series I (Special), failed to return from Kassel. (77 Squadron records)

Chapter 8

Berlin or Bust

Target bombed through cloud from 20,000 ft. Fires seem to be burning and glowing through clouds. Very heavy, intense and accurately predicted flak over target, also much fighter activity.

Entry in Log Book of F/O Philip Wadsworth for a Berlin raid

Apart from the celebrated Peenemünde raid, August 1943 had been taken up in raids on Italy – Milan and Turin principally – a policy which worked as Italy surrendered to the Allies on 8 September 1943. Bomber Command, and the grisly portent of Hamburg, had played their part. Now the bombers and their Commander in Chief could turn to Berlin, the 'Big City', the third largest city in the world, sending out three raids in the period between 23 August and 4 September.

On the night of 23 August 1943, 727 aircraft raided Berlin, and lost 56, a crushing 7.9% of those sent out. Defences were fierce, with wide belts of searchlights and flak, and hundreds of enemy aircraft, released from being tied down to their particular 'box' to await a straying *Tommi* and liberated to pursue their own course visually with the *Wilde Sau* technique.

A Master Bomber was provided for the raid – W/C J.E. 'Johnny' Fauquier, CO of 405 (PFF) Canadian Squadron, who had made his debut in Yorkshire at Pocklington. He was a flight commander of 'B' Flight on 405 Squadron, and had piloted a Wellington on the disastrous raid on Berlin of 7/8 November 1941. Later he would become a celebrated CO of 617 Squadron.

Despite the losses, the raid of 23 August 1943 was the most successful that Bomber Command had mounted so far. Many of the bombs fell on the edge of the city, and on the southern suburbs, but significant damage was done to the industrial areas of Mariendorf and Tempelhof, nearer to the centre of Berlin.

Yorkshire-based squadrons lost heavily. This time it was 4 Group's turn to pay the price, with 17 lost as opposed to 6 Group's five. P/O Bill Elder, a New Zealand pilot, had a hair raising time attempting to land back at Holme-on-Spalding Moor, with a fierce cross-wind blowing over the runway. He skimmed the top of a hawthorn hedge and nearly missed a house. As this was his second near fatal landing in a month (he had crash landed after one of the Hamburg raids) he found himself screened from operations after he emerged from his hospital treatment.

A Lancaster of 408 Squadron takes off from Linton-on-Ouse in August 1943. This aircraft was lost in a raid on Berlin 26/27 November. The CO of the squadron, W/C A.C. Mair was the pilot, and was killed. (408 Squadron records)

The crew of one of the five Breighton aircraft to be shot down also had an eventful time. It had been badly shot up by night fighters, and the pilot F/O Austin made a valiant attempt to reach Breighton. It was not to be. He died when the Halifax crashed into the sea, and the rear gunner, Sgt Russell helped the three surviving members of the crew, all of them injured, to board and cling to an empty fuel tank. Help was still 16 hours in coming. Sgt Rowen and Sgt Thewlis meanwhile died from their wounds. Sgt Russell, the only uninjured man and who had made such strenuous efforts to assist his comrades, was awarded a DFM.

There were a large number of POWs from the five Lissett Halifaxes of 158 Squadron shot down – 16 in all. P/O Frisby, RAAF, had nearly finished his tour when he was captured, and a call of a different kind was made upon his latent gifts and talents. He equipped with maps and documents many of those who made the 'Great Escape' breakout from Stalag Luft III at Sagan. His reputation as a forger of documents was unrivalled.

Between 23 August and 4 September 1943 three raids were made on Berlin, but there was not such a concentration of the bombing as was achieved at Hamburg. Furthermore, Berlin was not by any means an ideal H2S target. To get a good H2S picture, you needed to fly the

bomber straight and level. 'But straight and level over Berlin was suicide,' an aircrew member remarked. In one case where a brave and zealous pilot determined to provide the conditions for a good H2S image and flew the bomber straight and steadily as they neared the first set of Berlin defences, the rear gunner remarked in plaintive tones, after five minutes of this, 'Couldn't we weave, skipper, just a teeny, weeny bit?'

The second Berlin raid of this period was on the night of 31 August/1 September, with 622 aircraft sent out; Halifaxes, Lancasters and Stirlings. Forty-seven were lost. The Stirlings were hacked from the sky, 17 of them, 16%

Halifax crews enjoy a post-operational breakfast after a Berlin raid, 1 September 1943. (78 Squadron records)

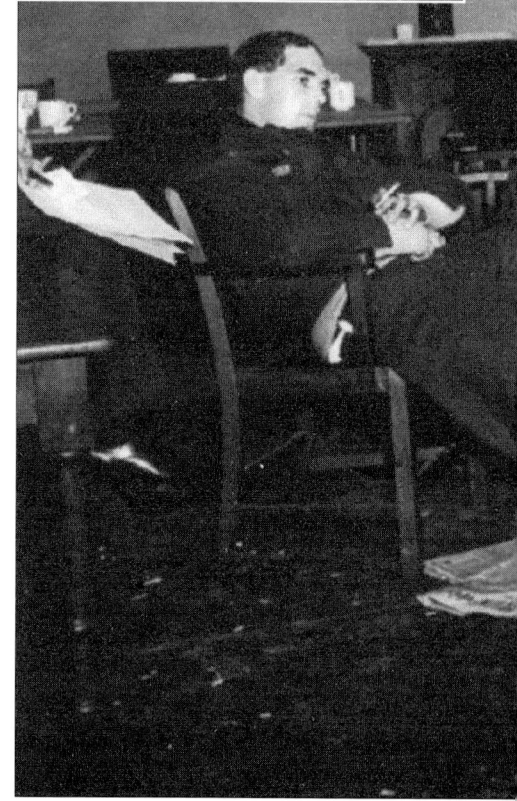

of the 106 sent out. There was difficulty this time with the H2S equipment, and the Pathfinders' markers seemed to go down well to the south of the target area.

Lissett, which had lost five aircraft on the last Berlin raid, lost four on this one. From the aircraft piloted by Sgt K. Ward, the flight engineer baled out safely, as did three other members of the crew, who became POWs. Sgt Simister, who evaded and got back to this country, received a Military Medal in 1945.

The third and final Berlin raid of this phase was on 3/4 September 1943. This attack was mounted

CO and crew of 78 Squadron at Breighton wait for debriefing on return from Berlin, 1 September 1943. (Graham Pitchfork)

by 316 Lancasters with four Mosquitoes. Nevertheless, 7% of those sent out failed to return, 22 aircraft. No aircraft from the Yorkshire-based 4 and 6 Groups took part in this raid.

There was now a two-month break from Berlin. Improved versions of H2S and other electronic aids were anticipated, and Bomber Command had lost an astonishing 125 aircraft and crews in three Berlin attacks.

Between the first and second Berlin raids, on 27/28 August, a raid on Nuremberg had been mounted by 624 aircraft. Thirty-three failed to return, including eleven Halifaxes from 4 and 6 Groups in Yorkshire. One of the Halifaxes lost from Lissett had its name painted on the side, *JAFBO*, an acronym for 'Just About Feeling Browned Off'. The people of Redcar on the Yorkshire coast had raised the money and paid for the Halifax in their 'Wings for Victory' appeal.

Also before the second Berlin raid on the night of 31 August/ 1 September, there was a 'double' raid on Mönchengladbach and Rheydt, with Pathfinders transferring the marking from Mönchengladbach to Rheydt after a two minute pause, a quite successful manoeuvre. Twenty-five aircraft, however, were lost, including three 76 Squadron aircraft from Holme-on-Spalding Moor, and three 78 Squadron aircraft from Breighton. Pocklington lost two, and 158 one. Six 6 Group aircraft also failed to return. Two 466 Squadron Wellingtons from Leconfield collided with each other on the outward journey.

Pathfinder marking was good on a raid on Mannheim and Ludwigshafen on 5/6 September 1943 and there were five heavy attacks made upon Hanover in September and October 1943, two very successful ones against Kassel, and still more raids on Mannheim. In the raid of 22/23 September on Hanover, a 76 Squadron Halifax, one of two lost, was shot down. It was captained by Sgt Fjaervall of the Royal Norwegian Air Force, who was killed together with four others of the crew. Sgt Dennis, the mid-upper gunner, who became a POW, was taken to a Hanover hospital and owed a German surgeon his life and his legs, which were shattered. The surgeon showed such skill that the feared amputation was not necessary. Sgt Dennis was repatriated to this country in September 1944, a good story to come out of such a relentless and bitter war.

The Hanover raid of 8/9 October 1943 was the last time Wellingtons flew with main force Bomber Command. The last one to be shot down was a Wellington X from 432 Squadron, flying from Skipton-on-Swale, captained by F/S Baker, RCAF.

Marshalling yards and railway plant looking towards Italy and the main coastal line became the object of attention on the night of 11/12 November 1943 when 4, 6 and 8 Groups sent 124 Halifaxes and ten Lancasters to bomb Cannes. Five Halifaxes were lost, three PFF aircraft from Graveley, and the others from 4 Group.

One aircraft from Lissett and 158 Squadron was the victim of a night fighter. Here the pilot and the mid-upper gunner were killed, two became POWs and three evaded. It was the mid-upper's first operational trip, and he was only there as a replacement for the crew's regular mid-upper gunner who was sick that night. The flight engineer, Sgt Kenneth Skidmore, made his way from Northern France, where he had baled out, to the Spanish border, with a winter journey through the Pyrenees to Gibraltar and home, being helped all along the way by courageous members of the Resistance. He was the first evader from the crew to arrive home, in February 1944. The other two got back in July and September 1944 respectively. As well as his RAF escape kit, Kenneth Skidmore carried a pocket Bible, and found the Psalms invaluable during the course of his evasion. Kenneth was finally ordained as a Methodist minister after a teaching career culminating in posts as headmaster of schools in the north west of England. He has written about his evasion in an arresting book entitled, in good biblical style, *Follow the Man with the Pitcher*.

The resumption of raids on Berlin began on 18/19 November 1943, with an all-Lancaster force of 440, while a Halifax and Stirling force of 395 aircraft attacked Ludwigshafen. A few days later a mainly Lancaster force took off for Berlin on the night of 23/24 November. Two Lancasters from 6 Group were among those that failed to return. Both flew from Linton-on-Ouse. One of them, from 408 Squadron, was piloted by an American from San Francisco, F/O Bell, while the rear gunner, F/S Hiscock came from Que Que in Southern Rhodesia. Commonwealth crews included, Bomber Command and 4 and 6 Group were taking on the characteristics of the Foreign Legion.

Another Lancaster-only raid on Berlin was mounted on the night of 26/27 November, while on the same night a force of 157 Halifaxes and 21 Lancasters raided Stuttgart. A 408 Squadron Lancaster from Linton-on-Ouse had a very eventful time. The captain of the aircraft was F/S R. Lloyd, RCAF. Not long before reaching Berlin the starboard engine failed. Their aircraft was now losing height, but they still succeeded in

releasing their bombs. The starboard outer engine then, as if by magic, restarted, but, as if this were tempting fate, the intercom to the mid-upper gunner went dead.

That mid-upper gunner, Sgt Robert, was then wounded in the foot

when they were hit by flak over Magdeburg. The next item in this flight's catalogue of horrors was an attack by a Junkers Ju 88. The mid-upper turret was severely damaged, and the engine pressure to the starboard inner engine fell. The engine had to be feathered, i.e. shut down with the propeller stopped to prevent the fire spreading.

That was two engines packed up on one side of the Lancaster. The aircraft was becoming impossible to control but by some miracle Lloyd had got it across the North Sea. Over Fiskerton the starboard outer failed, and a malfunction occurred in the rudder trim mechanism. Lloyd ordered the crew to bale out, yet quickly countermanded the order when the escape hatch jammed. Eventually he managed to crash land the Lancaster on the edge of a sewage disposal plant, very near Lincoln. It was a happy ending to a terrifying story at the end of which the sewage disposal plant was balm from heaven.

Most of the Yorkshire Halifaxes, some 210 in all, were withdrawn from the next Berlin raid of 2/3 December because of the threat of fog forming at their home airfields. The Vale of York and the Yorkshire Wolds are notorious for this. All available Halifaxes, however, together with 307 Lancasters attacked Leipzig on the night of 3/4 December. This was a successful raid with a loss of 24 aircraft (six from 4 Group and nine from 6 Group).

A remarkable escape from the trials that beset his Lancaster on the journey to Berlin and back on that night of 2/3 December, was experienced by F/S Roger Coulombe of 426 Squadron, Linton-on-Ouse. Over Berlin his Lancaster was coned by searchlights. 'There were 60 or 70,' he said, 'and I felt completely blinded.' Diving the Lancaster, Coulombe reached a speed of 450 mph, 100 mph in excess of the permissible speed. It became well nigh impossible to pull the aircraft out of the dive. In the end he had to put both feet on the instrument panel and heave back on the controls with all his might, with assistance from the flight engineer, in order to level the aircraft.

There now began a duel with a Junkers Ju 88 on the port quarter. A violent corkscrew caused the bullets to pass by harmlessly; the fighter attacked from the starboard side, with the same result, yet another corkscrew. Five attempts the Ju 88 made to attack the bomber, and after the fifth the mid-upper gunner, Sgt Stan McKenzie, opened fire at 60 yards range and saw his tracer ammunition enter the belly of the aircraft, which dived away and was lost to view.

Avoiding other encounters with a Messerschmitt Me 109 and a Focke Wulfe FW190, Coulombe thankfully left the target area. Amazingly, all the crew were uninjured. But the Lancaster was in a poor way – the port inner engine and the radio were out of action, and damage had been done to the port tyre, the port outer fuel tank and the Lancaster's entire hydraulic system.

Between Berlin and landfall on the English coast the starboard outer stopped running and Coulombe shut down the entire engine, feathering the propeller to reduce the consequent drag. But the starboard inner engine was also losing power, giving only 1,000 rpm – to maintain height, Coulombe needed 2,400 rpm. By now they were nearing the English coast and a Mayday call was sent out. Fortunately they were about to overfly an airfield near the coast, and this hospitable American base illuminated all its runways for the stricken Lancaster.

Coulombe brought down the aircraft to a safe landing on one wheel. Next morning he discovered that the starboard wing of the Lancaster had finally collapsed. Coulombe was commissioned and awarded the DFC soon after this eventful night.

The 16/17 December 1943, the night of the next Berlin raid, was known as 'Black Thursday' since while 25 Lancasters were lost over the target, another 34 crashed in England in dense fog. No Yorkshire-based Halifaxes were involved in this raid. A few days later, however,

A battle-damaged 51 Squadron Halifax made it back to Snaith on 20 December 1943 after a raid on Frankfurt. One member of the crew, fatally wounded, died before the aircraft reached base. (51 Squadron archive)

on the night of 20/21 December, 650 aircraft (including 257 Halifaxes) raided Frankfurt. A diversion over Mannheim by 44 Lancasters and ten Mosquitoes had not worked and 41 of those that set out to Frankfurt were lost, 20 of them from 4 Group and ten from 6 Group. A Berlin raid was mounted at the end of the year, 29/30 December 1943, with disappointing results. Twenty aircraft were lost, including nine Halifaxes (five from 4 Group and four from 6 Group). That raid represented the halfway point of the air Battle of Berlin.

Raids were mounted on Berlin early in the new year of 1944, but bad weather kept the Yorkshire Halifaxes from operating until the night of 20/21 January when 769 aircraft were dispatched to Berlin, including 264 Halifaxes, and 35 aircraft failed to return. Seven Halifaxes were missing from Pocklington that night, and three from Holme-on-Spalding Moor. Furthermore, 434 Squadron in 6 Group at Croft lost three.

The next raid, on Magdeburg (21/22 January), was the costliest night suffered by 4 Group during the war. They lost 22 aircraft and 6 Group lost 14. Holme-on-Spalding Moor (76 Squadron) lost five that night, including one Halifax piloted by another of the irrepressible Norwegians. He was Lt Tor Anundskaas, and he and his crew, lost without trace, are commemorated on the Runnymede Memorial.

On the night of 28/29 January 1944, with 432 Lancasters, 241 Halifaxes and four Mosquitoes, there was a very effective strike on the 'Big City'. Fires were visible to returning crews for up to 200 miles away from the target. Eighteen 4 Group aircraft were lost, and 15 from 6 Group. Several squadrons had four aircraft missing, while of the 6 Group aircraft, there was a total of nine missing Halifax Vs from Croft.

Thirty out of 134 aircraft from 4 Group setting out on this raid turned back. One amongst many unhappy events of that night was due to the increased weight of bombs some Halifax squadrons were detailed to carry, an increase from 63,000 lbs to 64,300 lbs. One aircraft from 76 Squadron, Holme-on-Spalding Moor, clipped a tree on take-off and crashed two minutes later.

The Luftwaffe over Berlin on that raid, in addition to their single-engined 'Wild Boar' fighters, had twin-engined fighters and four-engined Focke-Wulf Condors dropping flares. One pilot spoke of how bright everything seemed, 'clear as day', and of how he saw aircraft to left and right of him explode on their bombing runs. Due to the extra weight of bombs carried, some aircraft ran out of fuel and their crews had to bale out.

After one night of rest, another Berlin raid of 540 aircraft took place on the night of 30/31 January, of which only 82 were Halifaxes – Marks II and V were excluded. The only missing Halifax that night was one from 422 Squadron of Skipton-on-Swale. The reduction in the weight of bombs carried, after the experience of the previous raid, saved many of the Yorkshire Halifaxes that night.

A well earned rest followed, and not one major operation was laid on for 13 nights. New crews arrived on their postings, and after all those losses, new aircraft were delivered by the Air Transport Auxiliary (ATA) girls. 'But isn't your job very dangerous?' an anxious mother enquired of her ATA daughter. 'Only on the ground, mother,' the daughter replied.

The night of 15/16 February 1944 was a maximum effort, with 314 Halifaxes out of 891 aircraft dispatched to Berlin. This was the first time that over 500 Lancasters and over 300 Halifaxes had been sent out in one raid. Among the 43 aircraft lost were 15 from 4 group and five from 6 Group. Two Halifaxes were from 640 Squadron at Leconfield. The squadron was a new one. It had been made up of surplus crews of 466 Squadron, already at Leconfield (they also lost two that night) and of 'C' Flight from 158 Squadron at Lissett. No 640 was the last wartime squadron to be created in Bomber Command.

After being badly shot up by a Junkers Ju 88 on the approach to Berlin, F/S Eaton of 76 Squadron ordered his crew to bale out. All did so and became POWs, except for Sgt Upton, the mid-upper gunner, who plunged into an ice-covered lake and was drowned. He had taken the place of Sgt Wallis, the regular mid-upper, who had been injured in a crash on take-off four days before. Such are the fortunes of war.

A Leconfield Halifax III piloted by F/O Barkley crashed in the small hours of the morning while over home territory north of Scarborough at Cloughton. The hills just outside Scarborough are 300 ft high. This was the difference between the Yorkshire bomber squadrons and others, that they had elevated ground to contend with in North and East Yorkshire, often in surprising locations. This, coupled with a tendency for fog patches to cluster in the hollows of these hills, spelled the end of many a good crew.

Again there was a rest period away from Berlin. Leipzig was raided on 19 February 1944 by 823 aircraft (including 255 Halifaxes). Seventy-eight aircraft failed to return, and of these, 34 Halifaxes were lost, 14.9% of those that set out and did not make an early return. Harris now withdrew Halifax IIs and Vs from participation in the bombing of Germany. By the summer all Halifax units would operate the improved radial-engined Halifax III.

Amongst the casualties were four 77 Squadron aircraft. One of them, piloted by an Australian, F/L Ellis, DFC, included in the crew a man

A 434 Squadron Halifax BIII returning to Croft from a raid on Sterkrade. (Peter Green)

from the Irish Republic, F/O Sullivan. His father was the notable advocate, famous in legal and forensic circles, Mr Sergeant Sullivan QC. Another Irishman was killed that night, F/O Holmes, piloting one of 158 Squadron's three missing aircraft. He was from Athlone, County Meath. Thousands of Irish citizens joined Bomber Command and many hundreds paid the supreme penalty. This was something the Germans, when they interrogated downed Irish aircrew, just could not understand. 'Our struggle is your struggle,' they would tell the Irish.

These casualties over Leipzig were the worst in Bomber Command so far, though the last Berlin raid in the Battle of Berlin on 24/25 March 1944 would come close to that figure and the infamous Nuremberg raid of 30/31 March was to exceed it. Although some important industrial holdings were damaged, three raids on Stuttgart were only moderately successful, as was the attack on 24/25 February on Schweinfurt, in support of an American daylight raid of the previous day. An outstandingly successful raid on Augsburg a day later, which completely destroyed the old town, was publicised far and wide by Goebbels and his Ministry of Propaganda as a classic example of 'terror bombing'. Even so 21 aircraft were lost.

In the final attempt on Berlin, on the night of 24/25 March, aircrew reported huge searchlight concentrations over the city, and much flak over the Ruhr. An unnaturally high wind that night of over 100 mph (a 'jet stream'), far exceeding what was expected, blew many aircraft and crews about. No 78 Squadron at Breighton lost six Halifax IIIs, the

Lt. Gen. R. Lane ('Shady' Lane), a Canadian officer who was a Flight Commander of 35 Squadron, and a CO of 405 (PFF) Squadron. (Graham Pitchfork)

P/O Cyril Barton, VC. (578 Squadron records)

Vigil for the Nuremberg aircraft: the searchlight on and the 'blood wagon' ready at Snaith for overdue aircraft. (51 Squadron archive)

worst losses so far of any squadron equipped with the mark. Leeming lost six, three from 427 Squadron and three from 429 Squadron. A new squadron, 578 from Burn lost three Halifax IIIs. One of the 158 Squadron aircraft on this Berlin raid sent a message at 2240 hours, saying that port and starboard engines had stopped. The Australian pilot, P/O Simpson, attempted a crash landing on the beach of the Norfolk coast at Ingham. Tragically, he had landed on a minefield, a mine blew up, and the entire crew were killed.

On this raid there was a Canadian Master Bomber, W/C Reg Lane, known as 'Shady' Lane, CO of 405 (PFF) Squadron at Gransden Lodge in Bedfordshire. He had served on 35 Squadron in its Yorkshire days before it moved to Graveley and PFF, when he went with it. This was now his third tour, the second with Pathfinders. Crews reported the general encouragement he gave as Master Bomber, with forthright North American denunciation of the enemy: 'These bastards wanted a war; now show them what war is like.'

And then came the Nuremberg raid, a failure, with its toll of 95 missing bombers undoubtedly Bomber Command's 'biggest chop night ever', in the words of one of the survivors.

P/O Cyril Barton from the new squadron of 578 at Burn near Selby, flew his Halifax back to England, badly damaged, after three members of his crew had baled out due to a misunderstanding. Lacking a navigator and a wireless operator, and blown further up the North East coast than expected, Barton needed to make a forced landing when the engines failed, having run out of fuel. Near Ryhope Colliery in Sunderland he made a crash landing, in which he died, the three remaining crew members being only slightly hurt. A miner on his way to work was sadly also killed. In recognition of the fact that Cyril Barton had done all he could to save his crew he was awarded a posthumous Victoria Cross, the only one in 4 Group and the only one in the Battle of Berlin.

On this Nuremberg raid 4 Group lost 20 Halifaxes, with three crash-landed and one written off, while 6 Group lost 14 aircraft (mostly Halifaxes). Snaith and 51 Squadron were the highest losers with five aircraft lost and one crash-landed near Oxford on return, extinguishing the lives of the entire crew.

The briefing before Nuremberg (30 March 1944) at 51 Squadron. S/L Peter Hill (Flight Commander) briefs. G/L N.H. Fresson, Station Commander, sits third from left front row. Snaith lost five aircraft and crews. Some of the men in this room would die within the next few hours. (51 Squadron archive)

Unhappily for Snaith, a party of journalists and newspaper photographers had been invited to the station that night to cover a 'typical' Bomber Command raid at a 'typical' bomber station. As the CO, W/C Ayling, was on leave a Flight Commander, Peter Hill briefed the Snaith crew. There is a poignant photograph of this briefing, in which a good proportion of the faces peering at the Flight Commander would, like the officer

51 Squadron Station Navigation Officer S/L P. Jousse, a Rhodesian, helps Yorkshireman Harry Bowling prepare charts for his first op. It was to be his one and only. He was killed.
(51 Squadron archive)

Vigil for the Nuremberg aircraft in the Control Tower: notice the anxious officer on the balcony. Five have failed to return. (51 Squadron archive)

briefing them, be dead within a few hours. Another photograph from Snaith shows S/L P. Jousse, a Rhodesian and Squadron Navigation Officer, helping F/O Harry Bowling prepare navigation charts for his first operational flight. He was in the crew of an Australian, F/S Brougham – his Halifax would not return, and he would be one of five members of that crew, including the pilot, to be killed. The navigator of one of the only three Halifaxes to return to Snaith that night, Sgt J.M. McCoss, tells of the gloom in the debriefing room when they returned from Nuremberg after a flight of 8 hours and 3 minutes. His pilot was P/O M.J. O'Loughlin, with whom he flew 32 operations (and three more with another pilot) before being screened in August 1944.

One interesting legacy of the Nuremberg raid has become part of the Bomber Command heritage industry. Two brothers, Fred and Harold Panton, have created a memorial to their elder brother, Christopher, who did not come back from Nuremberg. Christopher Panton was killed as a flight engineer in a Halifax III of 433 Squadron, from Skipton-on-Swale, piloted by an American of Danish extraction flying with the RCAF, P/O Neilsen (they called him 'The Mad Dane'). There is a fine painting of Christopher Panton in the mess canteen at what is now called the Lincolnshire Aviation Heritage Centre.

Debriefing after Nuremberg at Snaith. P/O O'Loughlin and crew.
(51 Squadron archive)

Chapter 9

Operation Overlord

'After you, Claude.'
'No, after you, Cecil.'

*Conversation overheard between
two bomber pilots during a daylight
operation, on approaching the target.*

The Nuremberg raid effectively drew a line underneath the Battle of Berlin. Not that Harris had failed, as some historians argue, he just needed more time. Losses had been tremendous, awesome even. But lessons were being learned, and a few more raids like those in the second phase of the Berlin battle since January/February 1944 would, in Harris's view, have tipped the balance.

It was not to be. D-Day was barely three months away, and now the Commander in Chief, Bomber Command was 'under Eisenhower', the Supreme Allied Commander, with responsibility for all air matters delegated to Air Chief Marshal Sir Arthur Tedder, Eisenhower's deputy. So from April 1944 onwards Bomber Command, in the new grand scheme of things, was pledged to attack targets in preparation for the Invasion of Europe.

On 17 April 1944 the 'Overlord' Directive from the Supreme Allied

P/O McDonald and crew of 466 Squadron pose for cameras on their return to Leconfield from Berlin on 21 January 1944. (466 Squadron records)

Commander called for an attack on rail communications, 'particularly those affecting the enemy's movements towards the "Overlord lodgement area".' The Transportation Plan (notice the Americanism), to be carried out as a preparatory phase of Overlord, imposed on Bomber Command both a tactical and a strategic role.

In support of this plan, railway yards and sidings were attacked at Lille and Villeneuve-St-Georges (9/10 April). Attacking multiple rail targets in northern France like this, Harris was able to send out smaller numbers of aircraft from different groups to three targets simultaneously. And so on the night of 17/18 April, while aircraft of 6 Group, together with others of 8 Group attacked Noisy-le-Sec, Halifaxes of 4 Group and Lancasters of 3 and 8 Groups raided Tergnier. Four Halifax IIIs of 6 Group failed to return from the raid on Noisy-le-Sec, while six were lost from 4 Group (including two from Snaith and two from Lissett).

Meanwhile German cities also received visits from the bombers. A raid on Dusseldorf on the night of 22/23 April 1944 led to losses of nine 4 Group aircraft and eight aircraft from 6 Group. The pilot of one

76 Squadron aircraft shot down that night, F/L Lemmon, was from Brazil. He had started on bomber operations almost a year before, and was already the veteran of one crash. A raid to Karlsruhe on 24/25 April also yielded its crop of casualties, including two from Breighton and one from Holme-on-Spalding Moor, as well as six Halifaxes from 6 Group.

A second raid on Villeneuve-St-Georges to bomb railway yards led to a single casualty from Breighton and 78 Squadron. Included in the crew was P/O D.P. Garroway, whose father G/C Garroway, OBE, had been killed in 1941 as Station Commander of Linton-on-Ouse, leading a team of fire fighters coping with the aftermath of a raid on the airfield.

On 27/28 April Lancasters and Mosquitoes of 1, 3, 6 and 8 Groups carried out a raid on Friedrichshafen deep in Southern Germany, while aircraft of 4, 6 and 8 Groups raided railway yards at Aulnoye and Montzen. My father, flying as flight engineer to G/C Eaton, DFC, the squadron CO of 156 PFF Squadron, was killed on the Friedrichshafen raid, along with the entire crew. Of the four 4 Group aircraft missing from Montzen, three were from Snaith and 51 Squadron. Croft and 431 Squadron lost four aircraft on the same raid. One of these contained six airmen who evaded, another had two evaders in the crew. There would have been more evaders in the last aircraft were it not for the fact that the escape line helping them had been infiltrated by a double agent.

There was a steady trickle of casualties from the French 'Transportation' targets. An American pilot, F/L Mead, RCAF, was killed on 8/9 May piloting a 431 Squadron aircraft from Croft. He was from Detroit. A tremendous number of Americans served in the RCAF and a large number of them died on active service. From the other 431 Squadron aircraft from Croft to go missing on this raid, one member of the crew, F/O Schubert, RCAF, who eventually evaded, was hidden by a bricklayer and his family until the Allies liberated that area of Belgium. Aircrew from two other Halifaxes shot down that night from East Moor and 432 Squadron also evaded. If shot down over occupied territory at this crucial stage of the war, when invasion was imminent,

W/C David Wilkerson with his flight engineer behind and wireless operator below.
(Hugh Cawdron)

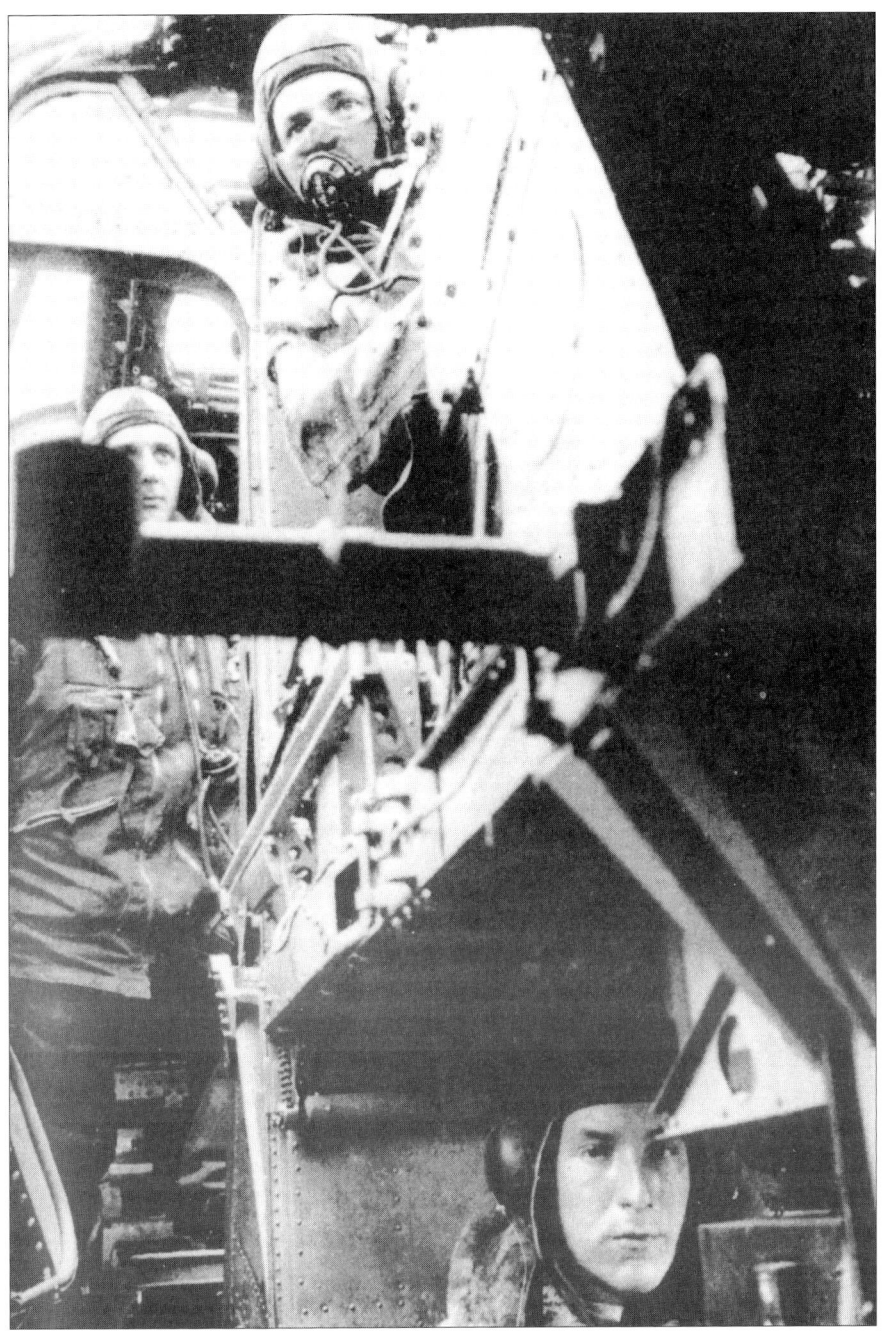

there were always at hand men and women of a certain calibre, ready to risk everything in assisting airmen on the run.

In the midst of such steady attrition and the destruction caused to the railway targets, on 22/23 May 1944, 361 Lancasters and 14 Mosquitoes raided Dortmund, the first large raid for a year. Three aircraft from 6 Group were lost: a Lancaster X from 419 Squadron at Middleton St George and two Lancaster IIs from 408 Squadron at Linton-on-Ouse. One of the latter was piloted by W/C Jacobs, DFC, AFC. He had commanded 408 Squadron since November 1943, after his predecessor W/C Main, DFC, had been killed in action. That same night three 6 Group aircraft, Halifax IIIs, were lost in a simultaneous raid on Le Mans, and one 77 Squadron Halifax V from Full Sutton in a force bombing yet another railway target in Orléans. Now Bomber Command was becoming a flexible and multi-tasked, multi-targeting instrument of war.

The 77 Squadron casualty was the first aircraft to be lost flying from the new aerodrome at Full Sutton near Stamford Bridge. It would not be the last. The squadron had moved there from Elvington in mid May, leaving Elvington for two Free French Air Force squadrons, 346 (Guyenne) and 347 (Tunisie), which conducted their first operations in June 1944.

On the night of 24/25 May 1944, 442 aircraft attacked two railway yards at Aachen, important links in the railway system between France and Germany. Eighteen Halifaxes were lost and seven Lancasters. From 158 Squadron at Lissett on this costly Aachen raid, five did not come back. It was a heavy night for 4 Group. Three 51 Squadron Halifaxes failed to return to Snaith and two to Holme-on-Spalding Moor. One of the Holme aircraft was piloted by F/S Wade, an Australian, with another Australian, F/S Graydon in the crew. There were considerable numbers of Aussies who served on 76 Squadron. Indeed, one of the ground crew was heard to comment to his mate: 'You're posted to this God-forsaken place, just north of the Humber, and the first thing you notice is people speaking English with a funny accent, the Aussies, and those who can't speak it at all, the Norwegians.' Another man, an aircrew member of the Sergeants' Mess on 76 Squadron, said he understood the

Pilot Neil Conway (RAAF) and crew outside their Halifax of 76 Squadron at Holme-on-Spalding Moor. Ernie Turtle, the flight engineer, is at the top of the pyramid.
(Ernest Turtle)

Norwegians, with their smattering of English, better than he did the Australians.

One of the three 51 Squadron aircraft missing on this night was piloted by an American, F/O C. McQuiston, USAAF, from Kansas. Nicknamed 'Tex', he played the guitar and was part of a Snaith Concert Party group. After he went missing over Aachen his talent as an entertainer was sorely missed.

In 40 days and nights a dedicated Australian pilot, Neil Conway, brought his crew from 76 Squadron and Holme-on-Spalding Moor through a tour of operations that took in transport targets in northern France (railway sidings), V-weapon sites also in northern France (Montorguiel, St Martin L'Hortier, Chateau Benapre, Nucourt), troop concentrations (Bourg Leopard, Villers Bocage), and synthetic-oil plants in the Reich (Bottrop, Rüsselsheim and Gelsenkirchen). Their tour, rapid, rugged and full of incident was a microcosm of the war Bomber Command fought at this period. F/L Ernest Turtle, the Flight Engineer, told the story of their tour to Jim Caborn, who wrote it up in the form of two articles headed '40 Nights' in *Flight* magazine for July and September 2000.

Asked to do a few more after they had reached the usual maximum 30 mark, the total operational tally of the Conway crew was 40. This reflects a period, with the shift to French targets, when the demands of the fluidly changing battlefield around Caen and Falaise were such that crews were being required to operate on short hauls twice in 24 hours in some instances. It was necessary, therefore, to keep some senior crews on for limited periods, so that these multiple demands could be fulfilled. It was a new experience for crews to finish tours and be posted away in such a short space of time.

Just before the Allied Invasion of northern France, the flight engineer in P/O Conway's crew was giving a brand new Halifax an air test.

Lancasters of 419 (Moose) Squadron at Middleton St George. The one in the foreground was shot down by a night fighter on the night of 1/2 May 1944 in a raid on St Ghislain. (419 Squadron records)

The motors cut, and Conway had to crash land the aircraft in a field. Apart from the rear gunner sustaining a blow on the head, the rest of the crew were uninjured. They missed flying over the invasion fleet to bomb Mont Fleury that night, but 24 hours later they were bombing targets at St Lô behind the Normandy battle area.

But make no mistake about it. These French targets were no milk runs. In April 1944, when Bomber Command was licking its wounds after Nuremberg and the Battle of Berlin, it was decided a French trip

counted for one third of an 'op'. Thus a trip my father made with other Pathfinders to Rouen on 18 April only counted for this absurd fraction, as did a raid on Laon on 22 April. Of the nine aircraft missing from Laon, one was from 77 Squadron at Elvington, captained by S/L Bond, a flight commander, and another was from 419 Squadron at Middleton St George.

After the raid on German troop concentrations at Mailly-le-Camp on the night of 3/4 May 1944, when 42 Lancasters were lost, it was considered that French targets counted for a full operation. 'I don't like these fractions in my log book,' my father commented to a friend at the time. But Mailly came too late for him. He was killed over Friedrichshafen five days after the Laon raid.

A few days before the Invasion, on the night of 2/3 June 1944, 128 aircraft raided the marshalling yards of Trappes. The outward leg passed without incident, but not long after leaving Paris the Luftwaffe night fighters pounced. It was a desperate battle as Halifaxes corkscrewed to avoid the Ju 88s. Fifteen 4 Group Halifaxes were lost. No 158 Squadron at Lissett had its biggest 'chop' night ever, with six lost. Two out of the six had a substantial number of evaders and POWs, but a lot of aircrew from that aerodrome near Bridlington were killed. Leconfield lost five Halifaxes, two from 466 Squadron and three from 640. In one of them, captained by P/O G.H.S. Burwood, the average age of the crew was 20. Attacks on these tactical targets, whether marshalling yards or troop concentrations, necessitated bombing at a low level. So, if the night fighter didn't get you, silhouetted below them by the light of the burning buildings, the light flak did.

A similarly costly night was experienced towards the end of the month of June (28th/29th) in an attack on railway yards at Blainville. Metz was also attacked that night by a force including some 6 Group aircraft, which made the Yorkshire casualties all the higher, twelve alone being lost in the raid on Blainville, six from 102 Squadron at Pocklington. Of the three missing from Holme-on-Spalding Moor, one Halifax piloted by a New Zealander, P/O I. McK. Weir (who became a POW), had a very experienced crew. The mid-upper gunner, Sgt Gregory, one of the two who lost their lives, had completed 47 ops, while most of the rest had flown between 31 and 39 ops. Seven 6 Group aircraft were lost, including two Halifax VIIs from 426 squadron at Linton-on-Ouse.

Two of the crew of one of the missing 426 Squadron aircraft were captured by the Gestapo and murdered, when they had been on the run for some time – P/O Birnie, RCAF, and P/O Jamieson, RCAF. Their deaths are reported as having occurred on 22 August, and they are remembered at Runnymede. The Halifax VII aircraft in which these brave would-be evaders were flying, piloted by another successful evader, F/L Logan, RCAF, was an improved version of the Mk III but with Hercules XVI engines fitted. All aircraft at Linton would eventually be equipped with the Mark VII.

It is as well to bear in mind the price some French families paid for sheltering or helping in any way downed airmen on the run. As the Allied forces gathered momentum and swept on to Falaise and south of Caen, as more and more shot-down airmen evaded, even so did the German authorities, and especially the Gestapo, adopt ruthless policies. Men, women, small children even, who assisted airmen would be executed or deported to labour camps or even concentration camps. Some evading aircrew, conscious of the debt they owed to these brave families, threw in their lot with the Maquis and fought among their ranks. Geoffrey Salisbury, an aircrew member of 76 Squadron, from Holme-on-Spalding Moor, wrote a stirring account of his adventures entitled *Yesterday's Flight Plan.*

A bomb aimer from 51 Squadron, F/O Harry Nock, parachuted from a stricken Halifax on 3 July 1944 and remained in the Ardennes area, working on the land and fighting for the local French Resistance. He was liberated by American forces. Until then his family thought he was dead.

Holme-on-Spalding Moor and 76 Squadron suffered particularly high losses during all periods of the war, as did 51 Squadron at Snaith, and 158 Squadron at Lissett. Not far out of this league was 102 Squadron at Pocklington, another heavy loser. A single, symbolic loss of a 76 Squadron Halifax on the eve of D-Day when they were out bombing coastal defence batteries at Mont Fleury and St Pierre du Mont made a great impression. The Halifax was captained by P/O Walker. All the 76 Squadron crews had followed the example of their CO, W/C 'Hank' Iveson in moving below cloud base to bomb, but it was too low for P/O Walker and his crew. The light flak got him and all perished.

This eve of D-Day, 5/6 June 1944 was indeed a jittery time. A Halifax of 77 Squadron setting out from Full Sutton failed to get airborne, and blew up. Miraculously the crew escaped with only injuries. A Halifax

from 578 Squadron at Burn was hit by flak after dropping his bombs on the Mont Fleury gun battery. The captain, S/L Watson, DFC, gave the order to 'bale out' while they were over the sea. He perished, together with three of the crew; the three who were rescued were picked up by a US Navy Tank Landing Craft, going to the D-day beaches. Returning crews saw the Invasion fleet spread out in the Channel below them.

A few days later on the night of 7/8 June, rail communications were attacked at Achères, Chevreusse, Foret du Cerisy, Juvisy, Massy-Palaiseau, and Versailles. Five 6 Group aircraft and six 4 Group aircraft were lost in the attack on Juvisy. A 466 Squadron Halifax, piloted by F/S W.R. Pearce, RAAF, became the first squadron casualty from Driffield. All the crew were killed on this, their first and only operation.

The first V1 flying bombs arrived over our coastline on 13 June 1944. Now Bomber Command turned its attention to launching sites and supply depots in the Pas de Calais area and beyond. Flying bomb raids took place on the same night as raids to other strategic targets. On the night of 16/17 June, for instance, 405 aircraft attacked four flying bomb sites. No aircraft were lost from these raids, except for a 10 Squadron Halifax which dived into the ground near Goole. The pilot was an Australian, P/O Leitch. Another Australian, F/S Coleman, was the only survivor.

Aircrew at Elvington being briefed. (77 Squadron records)

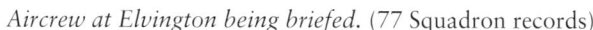

Night fighter aerial array on a Messerschmitt Me 110. (Peter Green)

That same night 321 aircraft, including some from 4 and 6 Groups, attacked the synthetic-oil plant at Sterkrade. This was a heavy loss night for Yorkshire-based squadrons. Of the 31 bombers shot down, 22 were Halifaxes. Full Sutton and 77 Squadron lost seven of its 23 Halifaxes dispatched. One crew, captained by P/O Judd, ditched off

149

Lowestoft after being badly shot up by a night fighter, and the crew were eventually picked up off Felixstowe. Another 77 aircraft, captained by P/O Crain, RAAF, exploded in the air. One crew member, W/O Owen, survived. The rear gunner, F/S Burns, an Australian like the pilot, had a brother who also died on active service. Australians did have their own squadrons, though not an entire Group like the Canadians, but large numbers of them served in most RAF bomber squadrons and many of them perished in action. The total number of Australians killed in Bomber Command was 4,050.

Pocklington lost five 102 Squadron Halifaxes that night against Sterkrade. Croft lost eight aircraft, four from 431 Squadron and four from 434 Squadron, a devastating setback. In one of the 431 aircraft, captained by F/O Blatchford, RCAF, was a F/O Carter who, while on the run, was captured and shot on 9 July. He is remembered at Runnymede. One of the missing 434 Squadron aircraft from Croft, piloted by F/S Haldeby, RCAF (who survived), lost three crew members including the flight engineer Sgt Ager, who at 18 was one of the youngest Bomber Command casualties.

German oil targets were at this time heavily protected by night fighters. The Reich only had synthetic oil and was being bled dry. Attacks on oil plants, therefore, often engendered high casualties, as in the case of the Sterkrade raid.

The first daylight attack made by 4 Group for over two and a half years took place on the afternoon of 22 June 1944. The target, a V1 bomb site at Siracourt in the Pas de Calais, was obscured by cloud and these 'ski-sites' demanded bombing at a low level. S/L McMullen, RAAF, and his all-Aussie crew of 466 Squadron, going low to bomb, were caught by flak and crashed. He was killed, at 22 an unusually young flight commander. No 466 (RAAF) Squadron had just moved to Driffield from Leconfield. Elderly Driffield townsfolk still talk about the 'invasion' of dark blue uniforms at the Buck Hotel and Keys Hotel in Middle Street, 'when the Aussies came'. Coming close to the Allied invasions in June 1944, this 'friendly invasion' was much appreciated.

Thereafter daylight raids were commonplace. But it could be an alarming prospect watching the Halifaxes jostle for position over a flying bomb site. A 10 Squadron crew were on their first 'op' to attack a flying bomb site at Montorgueil when the bomb aimer, F/S Arthur Smith witnessed a tragic incident taking place. F/S Kevin Gardner of a 76 Squadron Halifax piloted by P/O Neil Conway, and Sgt Ernest

Captured, and at Dyce airfield, a Junkers Ju88 C-6. (Peter Green)

Turtle, flight engineer in the same crew, also saw the incident, as no doubt did many members of the Group under these daylight conditions. A Halifax inadvertently dropped its bombs on another Halifax beneath it. The two aircraft were totally destroyed in the resulting explosions and their crews killed, one from 77 Squadron at Full Sutton and one from 102 Squadron at Pocklington. The navigator of the 102 Squadron aircraft had done his first 'op' around 23 June, very shortly before he met his end over the flying bomb site. A fellow navigator from Pocklington, on getting back from this ill-fated raid, noticed that the doomed navigator's log from his first op was open on his desk in the flight planning room. The Navigation Leader had written in fulsome terms upon the log: 'Good show. Keep this up, and you'll have no problem in completing a tour.' Such tragic ironies were an almost daily occurrence in the tough war the bombers fought.

The tragedy over Montorgueil led to the instruction being issued to Halifaxes to fly on daylight raids in loose 'vic' formations, to avoid collisions and being hit by another's bombs.

Daylight trips were flown especially in attacks on flying bomb sites. On the afternoon of 1 July 1944, 307 Halifaxes of 4 and 6 Groups with 15 Mosquitoes and six Lancasters of PFF attacked two launching sites at Biennais and St-Martin-l'Hortier. A 6 Group Halifax of 420 Squadron, having bombed the target at Biennais, made a crash landing at Linton-on-Ouse after both port engines failed – all the crew survived.

On the warm summer evening of 6 July, 551 aircraft took off to attack five flying bomb targets. Over one of these, Croixdalle, three 4 Group Halifaxes were lost. One, from Snaith and 51 Squadron, badly damaged by flak, was abandoned by its crew over the UK and all were saved. Another of the three, a 76 Squadron Halifax from Holme-on-Spalding Moor, had difficulty with its undercarriage and was instructed to divert to Carnaby, near the Yorkshire coast. Even with Carnaby's long emergency runway (9,000 ft by 750 ft, opened that year in March 1944) the aircraft overshot and ended up in woodland. The third Halifax had an unhappier story to tell. Returning home it crashed near Nottingham. All the crew died.

Bomber Command crews at this period had to be ready for any eventuality, from flying bomb or tactical battlefield targets on daylight raids, to old-style night attacks on synthetic plants. On the night of 20/21 July 1944 two 10 Squadron aircraft were lost on a trip to Bottrop,

W/C David Wilkerson, DSO, DFC. (Hugh Cawdron)

one of the synthetic-oil plants; two 51 Squadron aircraft from Snaith were also lost (although one of these came to grief on Woodbridge airfield in Suffolk, killing the three still on board). A 78 Squadron aircraft from Breighton went missing and, their greatest loss so far, six 578 Squadron aircraft from Burn.

No 578 had been formed as a new squadron out of Halifax IIIs from 'C' Flight of 51 Squadron at Snaith. Their CO, W/C David Wilkerson, DSO, DFC, who had been CO of 51 Squadron, led the new squadron to Berlin on the night of 20 January 1944, and also to Magdeburg on the next night, when one Halifax ditched off Flamborough Head and three members of the crew died of exposure before rescue came in the form of launches from Immingham. At length, W/C Wilkerson was posted away from the squadron, only to lose his life in an accident when a Martin Baltimore aircraft in which he was travelling as a passenger crashed. The funeral service was held at RAF Burn and this popular and much lamented CO, who got the very best out of those he commanded, was buried at Selby.

The loss of those six Halifaxes on 20/21 July 1944 was a massive blow to the new squadron, six months into its operational life. From one of the six, shot down in northern Holland, two crew survived. Another, piloted by an American from Seattle, F/L Couture, RCAF, was shot down by a night fighter, and the entire crew perished. Two Halifaxes among the six collided over the area of the village of

153

Balkholme, four miles north-east of Goole. Both were descending to the homeward stretch for a landing. Fourteen men perished. On 15 October 2005 a memorial to the airmen who lost their lives, with an interesting and vivid sculpture of two Halifaxes locked in collision, was unveiled and dedicated at the village of Balkholme. The maker and designer of the memorial, Hugh Cawdron, spoke of his involvement with the 578 Squadron Burn Association, deriving from his gratitude to and admiration of W/C David Wilkerson, who had been his Cub Scoutmaster in 1936 and a friend of his family.

Another stalwart supporter of the 578 Squadron Association is the squadron's Flight Engineer Leader who ended his second tour (his first was with 35 and 76 squadrons) in October 1944, F/L Jim Inward, DFC. As Engineer Leader, Jim was supposed to fly on ops once a month, but he actually flew whenever possible. He had had an exciting early war as a 19 year old. Sent out to Sweden by the Gloster Aircraft Company as a civilian, he and four other ex-apprentices of Halton found themselves at length located at various parts of the front in eastern Finland, instructing the Finns in the servicing of aircraft during their 'Winter War' with Russia. When the Finns surrendered on 13 March 1940, the beleaguered apprentices had a perilous journey to Helsinki and ultimately to Sweden and a return flight to England. Jim Inward later wrote: 'I still salute my Finnish friends, who treated as an oracle a 19 year old lad who was talking about an aircraft by reference to an English Instruction Manual and a quick assessment of the evidence in front of his eyes. The Halton training was paying a rich dividend. How I wished the pilots with whom we messed could have fought with Hurricanes and Spitfires.'

Attacks on V-weapon sites went on until 31 August 1944, and more and more demands were made on Bomber Command to assist with the battlefield situation. Meanwhile new squadrons were emerging and were feeding the system, continually fluctuating to match battlefield demands. As we have seen, 346 and 347 Free French Squadrons at Elvington had emerged, and in August 462 RAAF Squadron joined 466 at Driffield.

A trip to bomb the Opel car works at Rüsselsheim in August (12/13) was an old-style attack. Ernest Turtle, Neil Conway's flight engineer, reports exploding aircraft, flak all around them, and all the ingredients of a busy night. Two 76 Squadron Halifaxes failed to return to Holme-on-Spalding Moor from the raid, and a 102 Squadron aircraft from Pocklington, all the crew members perishing. There were also two 578 Squadron aircraft from Burn missing, in one of which the complete crew died. The other 578 Halifax, and the two 640 Squadron aircraft from Leconfield, that completed the toll of the missing that night, had a sprinkling of POWs and evaders, but the pilot in each case met his end. One of them was a 32 year old Wing Commander, W/C Maw, DFC.

From June 1944 right up into the autumn and beyond, the battle against synthetic-oil plants was waged with relentless ferocity on both sides. This was indeed the Nazis' Achilles heel, and the aim of Bomber Command, despite the Commander in Chief's remarks about 'panacea targets', was to 'turn off the tap'.

Pilot Harold Brown and his crew at Burn, mid-1944; Jim Inward (flight engineer) is third from the right. (Jim Inward)

Chapter 10

A Canadian VC and the War's Ending

Next to a battle lost, the greatest misery is a battle gained.

Duke of Wellington after Waterloo

In the late summer of 1944, 4 Group of Bomber Command were at the peak of their strength. Thirteen operational squadrons were flying from their East Yorkshire airfields, fully equipped with Halifax Mark IIIs.

We have touched earlier on the adventures of an outstanding senior officer in 4 Group, G/C John Whitley. In this last year of the war, on 12 February 1945, he was appointed AOC 4 Group, in succession to Air Marshal Sir Roddy Carr, and in May of the same year he became AOC 8 (PFF) Group. Gus Walker – Sir Augustus Walker – was another outstanding airman who found a home in 4 Group. While Station Commander at Syerston he lost an arm when a 'cookie' bomb exploded and he was trying to rescue trapped aircrew. He became eventually Senior Air Staff Officer at 4 Group, and endeared himself to Yorkshire-based airmen in the complex of aerodromes surrounding Pocklington. He is remembered at the Yorkshire Aviation Museum at Elvington where there is a room dedicated to him.

Another legendary 4 Group senior airman was the Station Commander

Sir Augustus Walker ('Gus' Walker), Base Commander of Pocklington and its satellite airfields. He lost an arm attempting to rescue a trapped airman from a blazing bomber. (Graham Pitchfork)

of RAF Holme-on-Spalding Moor, G/C James Pelly-Fry. He and the then CO of 76 Squadron, W/C Hank Iveson, DSO, DFC, had a unique partnership at Holme. Iveson was a robust Yorkshireman with a flying handlebar moustache, who exercised a considerable influence on those with whom he had to deal. Pelly-Fry had been Arthur Harris's personal

assistant in the late 1930s, commanded several bomber squadrons, led the raid by Bostons on the Philips factory at Eindhoven, and been equerry to HM King George VI. He was a remarkable blend of humour and authority, prefacing his remarks that were broadcast over the tannoy throughout the station in a manner reminiscent of a Butlin's redcoat – 'Hi de Hi! Pelly-Fry'.

6 Group, flying from North Yorkshire, was also in a fine state of operational fitness at this later stage of the war. In 1945 they fielded 14 operational squadrons, equipped variously with Halifax IIIs, and Lancaster Is and Xs. From February 1944 the AOC 6 Group was Air Vice Marshal Clifford McEwan, CB, MC, DFC and Bar. Because of a tendency to suntan quickly he had acquired the nickname in the inter-war years of 'Black Mike' McEwan. The nickname had a resonance about it, for he was a stickler for discipline and did not suffer fools gladly.

These were bomber groups where acts of significant courage in this relentless bomber war were commonplace. And yet, as is the case with 4 Group and Cyril Burton, VC, so with 6 Group; there was an outstanding act of valour and the award of a posthumous Victoria Cross. The VC was not gazetted until after the war in October 1946 but the act of valour occurred on the night of 12 June 1944, when a raid on Cambrai took place to destroy communications in the wake of D-Day. The award was made to a 27 year old Polish Canadian from Manitoba, P/O Andrew Mynarski, mid-upper gunner of a Lancaster of 419 RCAF Squadron flying from Middleton St George.

The Lancaster had been attacked by a night fighter and set on fire, with both engines failing. There was a raging fire between the mid-upper and the rear turret. On receiving the order to abandon aircraft, while he was going to the escape hatch, Mynarski noticed the rear gunner appeared to be trapped in his turret. Mynarski, without hesitation, made strenuous efforts to free his comrade, with the consequence that his parachute and clothing caught fire. Eventually the rear gunner signalled to Mynarski that he must now save himself. Mynarski reluctantly went back to the escape hatch, and stood to attention and saluted the rear gunner, still trapped in his turret, before diving out.

The rear gunner, by a miracle, survived to testify that had not P/O Mynarski turned back to help him, he would have been safe. As it was, Andrew Mynarski parachuted to the earth in flames, to be burnt so

P/O Andrew Mynarski, VC. (419 Squadron records)

Ruined German city – Dortmund 1945. (Graham Pitchfork)

severely that he died from his injuries. The pilot, rear gunner and two other members of the crew evaded and the story of Mynarski's heroism did the rounds. When the award was made in 1946 the world knew about it. Like Cyril Barton's action on the Nuremberg raid, it is an example of that 'greater love', a superb example of laying down one's life for one's friends.

For the middle part of the year 1944, Bomber Command was engaged in the relentless struggle against the V-weapons, and also the oil targets. The casualties in bombers shot down from mid-June to mid-August were 131, proving that the business of being bomber aircrew was still a deadly trade. By the time the last V1 crossed the English coast on 2 September 1944, anti-aircraft defences had virtually got the measure of these pilotless bombs. London and the south coast, however, and therefore Bomber Command, had no respite. For in a short space V2 rockets, which killed a total of 5,864 people in London and the south, were launched. Apart from the bombing of launching sites, the V2 threat was ended when the Allies overran these self same sites. The writing was on the wall for the German Reich.

That is why, apart from the necessary and inevitable assistance given to the troops on the ground and the Royal Navy upon the high seas, there were old-style area attacks on Germany. It was all of a part with bringing the Reich to its knees. Great damage was done to Bremen on the night of 18/19 August 1944 by a force of 288 aircraft. Only one aircraft was shot down, a Lancaster of 428 Squadron from Middleton St George. All except the rear gunner, F/S Good, mortally wounded and unable to leave his turret, baled out to safety.

On the night of 11 September Darmstadt was devastated by Bomber Command, mostly by 5 Group aircraft. Then came a directive against petroleum, transportation and armour, as primary bombing objectives. On 25 October, 771 bombers hit Essen again, and oil targets like Gelsenkirchen, Hamburg, Castrop-Rauxel and Sterkrade were sought after. Out of 22 operations, 14 of them were by day. The so-called 'second Battle of the Ruhr' took in a good many of the old targets. Dortmund and Bremen were pounded, and on 14 October, 1,013 Lancasters, Halifaxes and Mosquitoes bombed Duisburg. Four 6 Group aircraft were among the missing, a fraction of former tallies.

A 462 Squadron aircraft from Driffield experienced a catalogue of dangers the night of the Duisburg raid. P/O Cockerill's Halifax was coned by searchlights and almost torn apart by flak, just as he started his bombing run. Whirling fragments of shrapnel smashed into the cockpit, knocking the pilot unconscious and wounding him in the left eye. Down plunged the Halifax, out of control. P/O Cockerill recovered just in time, and badly wounded as he was, with blood pouring from his left eye and becoming weaker from loss of blood, he completed his bombing run and flew the aircraft back, making an emergency landing at Manston. During the landing Cockerill had to rely on another member of the crew to shout out the readings from the instruments, as by now he was almost blind. Thankfully, he was to recover completely. P/O Cockerill was awarded an immediate DSO. This was the only other immediate DSO awarded to a junior rank in 4 Group since P/O Leonard Cheshire's exploits over Cologne in November 1940, four years before. Cockerill's resolute action saved the entire crew, at considerable hazard to his own life. Driffield and the whole of 4 Group were hugely inspired by his brave action, carried out at the limits of his physical strength.

Heavier losses were sustained on an old-style area attack on Bochum on the night of 4/5 November 1944, when 23 Halifaxes and five Lancasters were lost. The roll call of the missing included three from Snaith, two from Breighton, two from Driffield, two from Leconfield and five 346 Squadron aircraft from Elvington. The French squadrons were suffering a severe attrition at this time. This was their worst night.

The pilot of one of the two missing Driffield aircraft had a very remarkable escape. F/L Joe Herman was flying with a crew which was, with the exception of the flight engineer, all Australian, and, just before reaching Bochum he was coned by eight searchlights. Violent manoeuvres shook the aircraft free. Maybe this was a bad omen – at all events Herman ordered his crew to clip on their parachutes. His own, however, stayed in the flight engineer's compartment, attached to a rack in the fuselage. There was no time for Herman to comply with his own instructions, he had to manage the Halifax, buffeted as it was in the slip streams of other aircraft. All too soon, his Halifax was coned again. And yet again Herman shook the aircraft free, and settled down on his bombing run. After releasing the bombs there was a change of course, and Herman plunged down from 16,000 ft to a lower altitude.

There was then a loud bang. They had been hit. The Halifax began to burn fiercely just behind the main spar, and Herman ordered the engineer to douse the flames. The engineer asked him if he wanted his parachute, and Herman asked him to put it on the floor of his (the engineer's) compartment. By now both wings were burning fiercely, and Herman gave the order to bale out. The rear gunner acknowledged, 'Going out', but the mid-upper gunner, 'Irish' Vivash sent a message, 'My legs are hit, skipper. I can't leave the turret'. Herman told him to get the engineer, Harry Knott, to help him. He was then just bending down to pick up his parachute pack when he saw the outer section of the starboard wing tear off. At the same time the Halifax went into a spin. Almost immediately there was a blinding orange flash, as the fuel tanks went up. There was now no roof and Herman, amidst a shower of debris, was flying upside-down into space. He had no parachute.

Joe Herman fell through the clear moonlit night, with dark objects falling all around him. He stretched out his arms to try to catch these objects. After all, one might be his parachute. He had fallen, in free fall, from 17,000 ft to 5,000 ft when instinctively he grabbed hold of something. To his delight he was gripping the legs of his mid-upper gunner, 'Irish' Vivash. This was only seconds after Vivash's parachute had opened. 'Irish' asked Herman to be careful of his right leg, which was broken. Inevitably the two comrades in arms landed heavily, although a tree, with outstretched branches cushioned their fall. Herman broke two ribs and damaged his hips, while Vivash had flak wounds in his right leg. The two of them, and Sgt Harry Knott the flight engineer, were the only members of the crew to survive.

When Joe Herman reached Stalag Luft III he wrote an account of what had happened to him, beginning 'This story is no line shoot'. He also told the story to a Sydney journalist he met in the prison camp, F/L Paul Brickhill (author of the celebrated *Dam Busters*), who included Joe Herman's amazing story in *Escape to Danger*, published in 1946. Had 'Irish' Vivash's parachute not opened late, Joe Herman would have accelerated in his fall past him, and plunged to his death. His survival had indeed been by a hair's breadth.

Of the other Driffield aircraft from 466 Squadron only the pilot, P/O N.C.R. Dodgson, survived. The Aussie squadron at Driffield was going through a baptism of fire, as indeed were the whole group, for 17 of the missing Halifaxes were from 4 Group. From one of the three Halifaxes missing or written off from Snaith and 51 Squadron, captained by F/S Berry, Sgt Peter Hinchliffe and Sgt Davis baled out. They were shot down on their return journey over Luxembourg. Peter Hinchliffe's girlfriend and future wife, a WAAF teleprinter operator at Snaith was most relieved to see him come back to 51 Squadron, all the more since it had been her painful duty to send out telegrams to next of kin reporting aircrew as missing.

The aircraft of F/S Berry had the image of a topless lady, designated 'Winsome Waaf', painted on the nose in the style of the celebrated American Vargas girls painted on the noses of B-17s. Authentic nose art though this was, the image was painted on a detachable sheet of canvas stuck on to the nose of the aircraft with adhesive tape. In that way the motif could be carried by a number of aircraft. F/L Freeman of 51 Squadron is portrayed in a photograph saluting 'Winsome Waaf' on completion of his tour, while a 51 Squadron crew in another photograph is shown standing by an aircraft with a different topless lady image, but called 'Winsome Waaf' nonetheless. Like all things in Bomber Command, the image was 'lucky for some' and not for others.

At the end of the year, 1944, there began an attack on the rail system that supplied the German Front, now under pressure from the Allies advancing from the east and the west. These tactical targets paid off, as indeed they had done in the softening up of communications prior to D-Day.

As a part of these attacks on Germany's rail system there occurred on 13/14 January 1945 an attack on Saarbrucken, in which a 51 Squadron Halifax from Snaith had its nose entirely shorn off in a mid-air collision with another Halifax from 347 Free French Squadron at Elvington. F/O Wilson was the pilot, and the aircraft was on the home run when the incident happened. Near Paris he noticed another Halifax a little too close for comfort on the starboard beam. Wilson instructed the mid-upper gunner to keep a particular watch out for it. Yet in a moment, the aircraft in question was on a collision course with Wilson's Halifax, and the two collided with a tremendous crash. The other Halifax, minus its tail fell away and disappeared into the night.

Wilson fought the controls to keep his Halifax in the air. It fell 1,000 ft before control was regained. Damage assessment revealed that the nose section of the fuselage just beyond the rudder pedals had completely disappeared – and the navigator and bomb aimer as well. The cold was

F/O Andrew Wilson of 51 Squadron loses 9 ft from his aircraft in a collision,
13 January 1945. Nevertheless the Halifax is brought back to an English airfield.
(Hugh Cawdron)

Lancaster QB-P, Piccadilly Princess, of 424 (Tiger) Squadron. This squadron first used Lancasters operationally on 1/2 February 1945. (Peter Green)

intense and cruel, and sparks were flying about from shorn-off pieces of equipment. And yet the engines were still running on at cruising power. The dinghy had gone and the wireless operator's parachute was damaged.

F/O Wilson left the engines as set, and had all the electrics switched off to stop the coruscating sparks and lessen the risk of fire. There was no intercom working, so the gunners were brought up to the front to an area marginally warmer than their turrets. Experimenting with heights, Wilson tried to take the Halifax to 11,000 ft, whereupon it stalled. Reducing height, therefore, he continued at 7,000 ft. Over the English coast, Wilson issued a distress call. Welcoming searchlights pointed out the position of an airfield, that of Ford in Sussex, and Wilson made a good landing, on his second attempt, fast and low.

The other Halifax had lost three of its crew including the pilot, Adj E. Jouzier. Thanks to Wilson's coolness in his captaincy and presence of mind, the four remaining members of his crew and he himself were

saved. It was a notable achievement and a terrifying experience. F/O Wilson was awarded a DFC.

Another priority, urged on by Bomber Command, was what was known by the codename Operation 'Thunderclap', a plan to devastate cities in East Germany, packed as they were with refugees and yet at the same time acting as transit points for tanks and war material being delivered to troops holding the line on the Eastern front. Dresden, Leipzig, and Chemnitz, as well as Berlin itself, fell into this category.

Oil targets went on being attacked, before Thunderclap was put into operation, with devastating results to Dresden on the night of 13/14 February 1945. The Dresden raid was an all-Lancaster attack. Of the two separate waves that made up the attack of that fateful night, 6 Group aircraft took part in the second wave. Six Lancasters were lost, none being from the Yorkshire-based squadrons. It is estimated that between 40,000 and 50,000 of Dresden's residents lost their lives in the fearful firestorm of that night.

On another Thunderclap target raid to Chemnitz, on the night after Dresden, eight Lancasters and five Halifaxes were lost, the latter from 4 and 6 Groups in Yorkshire. Two of the 4 Group aircraft were from 640 Squadron at Leconfield, one of them piloted by P/O H.M. de Bij, a Belgian. It remained true throughout the war that more aircrew from occupied Europe served in the Yorkshire-based squadrons than in any others. We have seen the steady infusions of Norwegian aircrew at Holme-on-Spalding Moor, needing to be continually renewed against the background of severe casualties; there were the two Free French squadrons at Elvington, the Poles at Lindholme earlier in the war, and the occasional lone Czech or Pole or Belgian, like this one from Leconfield. The Canadians themselves in 6 Group were a regular melting pot of nations. British aircrew on the Empire Air Training Scheme in Canada testified to the babel of languages they heard in Vancouver and Toronto, not to mention up and down that vast country, where sometimes three separate Slavonic languages were being spoken in one small town.

Canadian crews were badly hit by a second raid on Chemnitz in the Thunderclap series on 5 March 1945, where the aim was, as in the Dresden and first Chemnitz raid, to cause dislocation and disruption of communications in the face of the advancing Soviet armies. Much of the damage and destruction suffered by bombers on this raid, however, was due to the weather. Three of 426 Squadron's Halifaxes from Linton-on-Ouse crashed while taking off for Chemnitz in mid-afternoon, due to heavy icing. One crashed near Hutton-le-Hole and exploded, while another collided with a 425 aircraft from Tholthorpe; both came down near Nun Monkton and there was only one survivor, F/S A. De Cruyenaere from 425 Squadron. In all, seven Halifaxes crashed, within minutes of becoming airborne.

The worst of these incidents was that of the Halifax, again from 426 Squadron and Linton-on-Ouse, that in common with many others encountered severe icing and broke up, when flying over York. Six crew members were killed and five civilians died also, as an engine sliced through the roof of a local secondary school and wreckage was scattered all over Nunthorpe Avenue. From the doomed aircraft only the wireless operator, P/O Low survived. Even so, his survival was nothing short of miraculous. At such a low altitude his parachute could not be deployed, but blast from the exploding bombs (they had only just set off, remember) pushed him upwards to a height where his parachute could open properly.

There were other casualties that night, both over the target and on the return, when icing was again encountered. A Pocklington aircraft, off course, crashed in Czechoslovakia, and a 432 Halifax from East Moor was shot down by friendly fire from one of our coastal batteries, with all the crew killed. Two 10 Squadron aircraft from Melbourne were shot down, while two aircraft from 578 Squadron at Burn came to grief on return at Bovingdon airfield in Hertfordshire, with one already parked and the other running into it. Fortunately the crews were uninjured, but it was yet another of the kaleidoscope of experiences the bomber crews suffered on that afternoon and night of horrors. All in all, 51 bombers were written off before, during and after the Chemnitz raid.

The night of Chemnitz was, in the main, a 6 Group tragedy. The previous night, that of 3/4 March, was a 4 Group tragedy, when 20 bombers were lost, all over England and none over Germany, out of 234 aircraft sent out to bomb Kamen. Of these, eleven were from 4 Group.

One Halifax from Driffield, back in the home circuit, had to seek an alternative landing ground as the airfield lights were extinguished due to the presence of an intruder. A Junkers Ju 88, however, shot down the Halifax and it crashed at Fridaythorpe, nine miles out of Driffield on

Lancaster of 420 Squadron at Tholthorpe, April 1945.
(420 Squadron records)

the main road to York. Four members of the crew were killed, including the pilot, P/O Shelton, RAAF, who is buried in Stonefall Cemetery in Harrogate, together with two other Australian members of the crew. The crew of another Driffield Halifax had a happier story to tell that night. Attacked on their return to Driffield, all managed to bale out safely.

Three Free French Halifaxes were among the victims that night of Operation Gisella – a massive intruder operation by 200 Luftwaffe fighters. Approaching Elvington, one, from 346 Squadron, was diverted to Croft, but was shot down by a Junkers Ju 88 near Darlington. Four of the crew were injured, and two civilians were killed when the stricken aircraft, in flames, slithered along the ground. Another Halifax was shot down by an intruder aircraft near to RAF Cranwell in Lincolnshire. Five of the crew baled out safely but the pilot, Capt Laucou, stayed at the controls and tried, unsuccessfully as it happened, to achieve a safe crash landing. The flight engineer, Sgt Masson, had been severely wounded and so was unable to bale out. Both perished in the crash. The second 347 aircraft came down seven miles from York, near Sutton on Derwent, also the victim of a German intruder. Six managed to bale out to safety but the body of the pilot, Lt Terrien, was discovered near the wreckage of the Halifax.

It was a costly night. Eleven Halifaxes from 4 Group were shot down, with six more damaged. But this was the Luftwaffe's swan song, her last major effort, a final pre-emptive strike. It met, however, with a vigorous response from the RAF. These last few operations in the war generated a crop of deadly and sometimes surprising casualties. A daylight raid on Essen on the morning of 11 March 1945 had the largest number of aircraft sent out since the war began, 1,079. Three Lancasters were lost, two from Croft. One was from 431 Squadron, and was piloted by the squadron CO, W/C Davenport, who was killed. The other Croft aircraft was from 434 Squadron. Hit by flak just after finishing its bombing run, the pilot, F/L Fern, and five of the crew were killed. For the rear gunner who survived, there were many years of hospital treatment ahead.

In a raid on Hamburg on 31 March the new German jets were out in force and accounted for six 6 Group aircraft. Some aircrew became POWs – they would not have to wait long for liberation. On 4/5 April 1945, the Rhenania oil plant at Harburg was targeted. Two Lancasters

Crew of 10 Squadron at Melbourne in March 1944, with an American style pin-up on the nose of their Halifax. (10 Squadron records)

were lost, and a Halifax from 78 Squadron at Breighton. The mid-upper gunner, P/O Burns, was an Irishman from Curragh, County Kildare in the Republic, among the last of that prodigal outpouring of comradely sacrifice that came from the Irishmen of Bomber Command, and which so disconcerted those who wished to distance themselves from the British, the Commonwealth and their war.

The last major Bomber Command attack took place on Hamburg on 8/9 April 1945. Seven Halifaxes and one Lancaster from 4 and 6 Groups were among those lost. A Breighton aircraft from 78 Squadron crashed near Pocklington (the high ground was a death trap in poor visibility around the town). The same conditions prevailed at Driffield where fog blanketed the airfield. The seven-man crew of a 466 Squadron aircraft all died after clipping some trees and crashing at Mr Megginson's farm at Kirkburn Grange, two miles west of the aerodrome. The captain of the doomed aircraft was P/O D.J. Watson, RAAF. This was sheer bad luck, and a great tragedy for their families within sight of the war's end.

F/L Freeman saluting the 'Winsome Waaf' nose picture on completion of his tour.
(51 Squadron archive)

The ill-fated Halifax, 'F for Freddie', had flown 96 ops when it crashed. The nose art on 'Freddie' portrayed the cartoon character Olive Oyl reproaching a crestfallen Popeye with an acronym spelling out the word G-U-T-S, decoded as 'Get up them stairs'. Psychologists would call it an interesting example of displacement therapy, to decorate an aircraft of dark and serious mien and intent like a four-engined bomber either with erotic motifs (cf. Snaith's 'Winsome Waaf') or with cartoons borrowed from contemporary culture. This process was endemic at Driffield and Snaith airfields, each of which possessed gifted practitioners of the art. One of Driffield's aircraft was nicknamed 'There Oughta be More Time for Love', and had painted on the nose a girl, soignée and elegant with a long dress. Happily the Halifax did 67 ops before she was struck off charge at the end of the war.

The crew of 'F for Freddie' were the last casualties from Driffield.

F/L Kemp and crew leaving 'Expensive Babe', 51 Squadron, Snaith.
(51 Squadron archive)

'There oughta be more time for love' – nose art on a 466 Squadron Halifax III at
Driffield. (466 Squadron records)

175

A Lancaster of 427 (Lion) Squadron Fannin' Fanny 1945. Struck off charge in October 1946. (427 Squadron records)

From this airfield the squadrons had born the brunt of early Bomber Command losses from the outset of war and those endless leafleting raids, to the last operations of these two gallant squadrons of the RAAF in the hectic closing stages of the war.

March 1945 had seen the use of the elongated runway at Carnaby near Bridlington by 617 Squadron, to practise taking off with the Grand Slam bombs of 22,000 lbs before starting to fly from their home airfield of Woodhall Spa. On 13 March two aircraft of 617 Squadron, after an abortive mission, brought their Grand Slam bombs back with

S/L Ted Eagleton, DFC, and crew stand outside their Halifax III, of 466 Squadron, 'Get Up Them Stairs'. It had done 91 ops. On the 96th op it crashed with another crew and pilot in it two miles from Driffield aerodrome. All were killed, just a few weeks before the war ended. (Andy Thomas collection)

them to a landing at Carnaby rather than jettisoning them in the sea. The airfield, only opened the year before in March 1944, had known some excitement, not just because of its generous runways which were kind to stricken aircraft but on account of its FIDO system (Fog Investigation and Dispersal Operation) which enabled aircraft to get down safely in dangerous conditions. Another FIDO system had been installed at Melbourne aerodrome, home of 10 Squadron. On Boxing

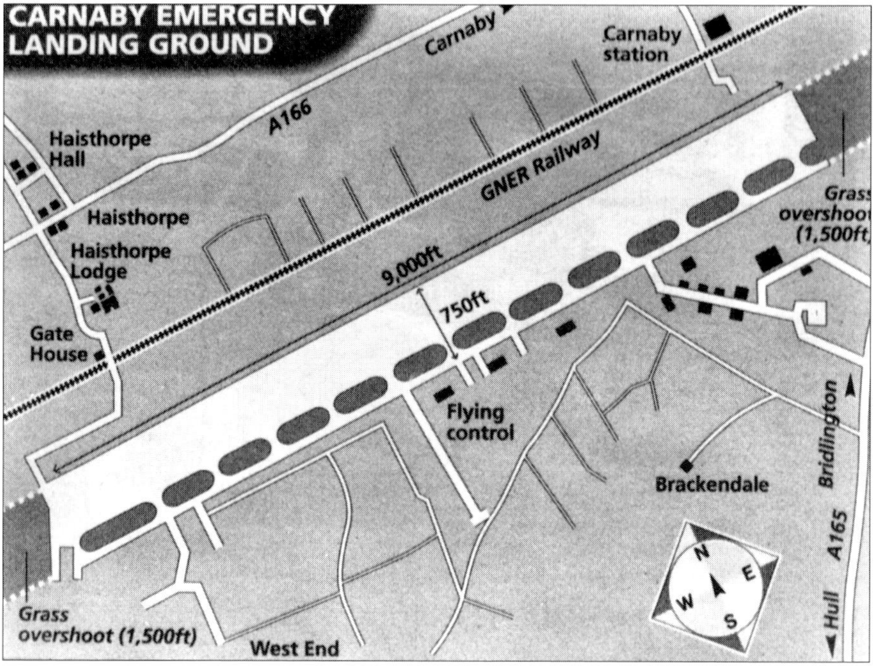

Map of Carnaby Emergency Landing Ground (near Lissett, Bridlington and the North Sea). (Peter Green)

Day 1944, 20 Halifaxes got down in severe fog at Carnaby, but the incident to end all others came in late January 1945 when 65 bombers of the USAAF (mostly B24s) made the landing here after being diverted to Carnaby from an aborted raid on Brunswick. Carnaby was well placed for limping bombers and anxious crews, being only a mile from the North Sea. Local folk speak of far more 'narrow escapes' surrounding this airfield than got into the official records. They are, it must be emphasised, extraordinarily alive even in this present day to the echoes of the bomber war coming to them from over 60 years ago.

A large number of aircraft, 969 from all bomber groups, attacked the naval base on the small island of Heligoland on 18 April. Seven Halifaxes were lost, all from 4 and 6 Groups. From four of these bombers the entire crews were safe. In the case of the remaining three aircraft all perished, and most of the names are on the Runnymede

Memorial. One of these three, a 640 Squadron Halifax from Leconfield, captained by P/O Pugh, RAAF, had another Australian in his crew, W/O Franklin, and F/S Whittenburg from Nairobi, Kenya. What journeys these aircrew made before giving their lives, so far from home, like this young man from Nairobi, three weeks before the end of hostilities!

The last raid of the war for aircraft of 4 and 6 Groups was on 25 April 1945, designed to destroy the coastal batteries on the Frisian island of Wangerooge, which dominated approaches to Bremen and Wilhelmshaven. The supreme tragedy of this last raid of all was that six out of the seven losses were through mid-air collisions. Crews were tired and levels of alertness were not at their best, for the weather was very clear. Smoke and dust produced an artificial pall over the target. From these six aircraft only one aircrew member survived, the pilot of one of the 76 Squadron aircraft, P/O Lawson, RCAF, who succeeded in pushing himself clear from a position trapped in the wing as his Halifax dived towards the North Sea. He landed unhurt in shallow water to become another short-term POW. The only aircraft shot down on this raid was from 347 Squadron at Elvington. Captained by Sgt Mercier, its crew were the last Free French to be killed in the war.

After such a tragic final operation there was to be no more 'dicing with death' for the two Yorkshire-based bomber Groups. Men who

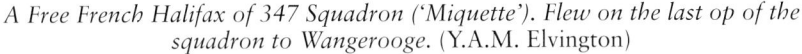

A Free French Halifax of 347 Squadron ('Miquette'). Flew on the last op of the squadron to Wangerooge. (Y.A.M. Elvington)

did not expect to live, who wrote themselves off, especially after the experience of these last few deadly operations, now had a lifetime ahead of them. 'It was like being born again,' one of them told me, and he was not speaking within a religious context. Aircraft of 5 Group began to ferry home prisoners of war, others dropped supplies and food to a starving Dutch population, while a final operation on 2 May against Kiel saw the very last wartime casualties. And so the Germans surrendered unconditionally on 7 May, and Tuesday, 8 May 1945 was a public holiday – VE Day.

Chapter 11

Remembering

Their bodies are buried in peace; but their name liveth for evermore.

Ecclesiasticus 44:14

After the victory, after the cessation of hostilities, the realisation of loss, tremendous loss. Between 1939 and 1945, 55,888 aircrew in Bomber Command were lost out of a total of 100,000. From Bomber Command in the Yorkshire squadrons, 4 Group in the East Riding flew 57,407 sorties, for the loss of 1,509 aircraft. 6 Group, who, remember, were not formed until 1 January 1943, flew 39,584 sorties for the loss of 784 aircraft. Thus at 18,000 lost aircrew the Yorkshire squadrons supplied just under one third of Bomber Command's total fatalities.

This was indeed an appalling price in blood. 4 and 6 Groups suffered grievous casualties, especially the Halifax squadrons. It is not an overstatement to say that, with their altitude threshold being 2,000 ft lower than that of the Lancasters, the Yorkshire Halifaxes were hacked from the sky in the air Battle of Berlin. And yet 460 Squadron from Breighton near Selby (although at the time in 1 Group and flying Lancasters), was the squadron that lost the most aircraft and aircrew in the Battle of the Ruhr. One of 460's Lancasters, 'G for George', serialed W4783, had a long life at Breighton from December 1942 and afterwards at Binbrook in Lincolnshire, the squadron's next home, and was subsequently presented to the Australian War Museum in Canberra where it remains to this day.

There were seven Yorkshire Halifaxes which bucked the odds, despite the fearsome attrition that made twelve trips the average for each machine, and achieved the remarkable distinction of '100 Not Out'. Halifax Mark III LV907 was sent to Lissett in March 1944 and flew for 128 operations, the last one being in the fateful skies of Wangerooge on 25 April 1945. Another Halifax, LV937 'E', of 51 Squadron at Snaith, with a piece of meretricious nose art portraying the aircraft's nickname 'Expensive Babe', did well over 100 operations and survived to be struck off charge in July 1945. Yet another Halifax, MZ527 'W', at Burn and in 578 Squadron, achieved this remarkable distinction, as well as another dubbed C-Clueless, which was with 158 Squadron at Lissett. C for 'Clueless'? If ever an aircraft was ill named, after such a long and charmed life, that was it.

Looking back at some squadrons in our Yorkshire air bases that seemed to hold a record for heavy losses, and concentrating on their period of worst loss at the time of the Battle of Berlin, we single out for mention 77 Squadron from Elvington, near York and 78 Squadron from Breighton, near Selby, 102 Squadron from Pocklington, near York, and 158 Squadron from Lissett, near Bridlington and the North Sea. All these squadrons lost 16 aircraft at the time of the Berlin air battle, as did 426 Squadron in 6 Group from Linton-on-Ouse, which had the distinction of flying Lancasters all through the Battle of Berlin, and being equipped with Halifaxes from April 1944 until the war's end.

Turning from crippling casualties and the astonishing operational totals of the lucky few Halifaxes, it must be said that 4 Group, Bomber Command was an original night bombing group. Its Whitleys were there dropping leaflets on the first night of the war in 1939. Now there was a lot wrong with the Whitley, in the light of later development of heavy bombers, but it was a good stand-by for Bomber Command in the early years, with the rugged structure required to accommodate the stress of the bombing campaign. This tradition in 4 Group of 'taking the strain' and 'bearing the brunt' was continued by the Halifaxes, which, despite their lower altitude threshold, were able to take an enormous amount of punishment.

The airfields one passes on the Yorkshire roads, some of them operational still, many of them derelict, are a real focus for memories of the air war. A trip up the A1 evokes those aerodromes in North

Leeming camouflaged, with a Whitley V. (Peter Green)

Yorkshire that were flanked or bounded by the Great North Road, as it was then called – Leeming, Dishforth or Middleton St George, the most northerly of bomber stations, where returning crews scanned the darkness for the white ribbon of the Darlington to Saltburn road. Coming in to Pocklington, crews looked for the school buildings at the edge of the town, the gleaming line of the canal, and the spire of the church at Barmby Moor. At Melbourne crews had to be careful to avoid the black bulk of the windmill at nearby Seaton Ross, while at Holme-on-Spalding Moor the tangle of little lanes just beyond the airfield was visible as a kind of dark chequerboard in the night gloaming, signposted in the village in daylight as Land of Nod, a name as old as the book of Genesis.

Returning Lissett crews looked for the comforting presence of Flamborough Head projecting out of the North Sea to find the airfield south of the Head, two miles to the west. If they inadvertently went

Halifax coming in to land at Melbourne. Note Seaton Ross windmill.
(10 Squadron records)

too far to the west, they could easily become entangled in the Driffield circuit a few miles further on.

The old airfields should indeed be a place for remembering. After all, for the wartime aircrew it was here on the airfield that they had a short life, here that they flew together, and went out in the liberty bus together to the nearest town. Sadly, in all too many cases it was from here that they flew out to die together. The squadron Operational Record Books use a terse euphemism opposite the names of a missing aircraft and its crew: 'Nothing heard of this aircraft since take-off'.

So that the airfield, a place of gathering, and riotous celebrations on stand down nights, that place where this little family of seven slept and talked, is the place to claim their presence rather than the war cemetery, or the target or anywhere on the long flight path, outward or returning. Not surprisingly Richard Holmes, author and broadcaster, in his book *Battlefields of the Second World War* calls the airfields 'unutterably poignant places'.

In Yorkshire, with lots of open country and open skies, airfields are very much part of the landscape and, of course, some airfields have been put to other uses. Middleton St George is now Durham Tees Valley Airport, Pocklington houses the Wolds Gliding Club, Driffield is a massive Grain Store for the EEC, Full Sutton and Lindholme are used as HM Prisons. At Driffield also there are three roads on an industrial estate, a former part of the old airfield, which are called after wartime aircrew – Pexton Way, Wadsworth Way and Warfield Way. Wadsworth Way is named after my father, and Pexton Way after F/L Ben Pexton, DFC, a Pathfinder pilot who was at school with my father and who perished in one of the Hamburg raids of 1943. There is a memorial to him also in the form of a window in the parish church of Watton near Driffield, where his family have farmed for generations. Warfield was a post-war Driffield CO with a good wartime record, well known in town and district.

The former 4 Group airfield at Elvington near York, home of 77 Squadron for a great part of the war, has been for a number of years the Yorkshire Air Museum and Allied Air Forces Memorial, with many exhibits and invaluable archives. There is a special memorial to 346 and 347 Squadrons, looked after by members of the Free French Air Force. Within a T2 hangar is a Halifax Mk III, LV907 'Friday the 13th', the only example of a Mark III anywhere in the world. This aircraft actually completed 128 sorties by the end of the war, being flown with 158 Squadron at Lissett.

As the veterans grow older, many memorials have been dedicated to them, and serious attempts have been made to tell their stories, in the form of individual squadron histories. At Skipton-on-Swale

there is a Royal Canadian Air Force Memorial, and at Tholthorpe, to commemorate Canadian squadrons who served there, an avenue of oak and maple trees has been planted. At Melbourne a memorial has been erected at the entrance to the old airfield, and near Burn the Balkholme Memorial commemorates those men of 578 Squadron who lost their lives on 20 July 1944. At Snaith there is a Memorial Garden with a stone dedicated to the memory of 51 Squadron; there is a plinth on the old airfield at Pocklington recording and remembering the sacrifice made by members of 102 and 405 (RCAF) Squadrons; while in the churchyard of Lissett near Bridlington there is a plaque remembering 158 Squadron's tenure of the airfield and the sacrifices they made.

In the Garden of Remembrance in Driffield, made from grey granite hewn from a quarry near Eugowra in New South Wales, is a memorial that honours the 482 men of 466 and 462 (RAAF) Squadrons who gave their lives while they were flying from Leconfield and Driffield.

War graves at Stonefall Cemetery, Harrogate. Most of them belong to Canadian airmen who flew from Yorkshire airfields. (Yorkshire Air Museum)

Betty's Tea Room, home of the celebrated 'Betty's Bar' with its mirror, surviving to this day, on which wartime aircrew scratched their signatures.
(Yorkshire Air Museum)

In St Mary's church, Beverley there is a Book of Remembrance for 466 (RAAF) Squadron. There are memorial stones at the edges of many of the other 4 Group and 6 Group airfields.

In 1955 an RAF Memorial in the form of an astronomical clock was unveiled by HRH the Duke of Edinburgh in York Minster. Together with this clock, which reflects the skill of astro-navigation deployed by Bomber Command navigators, there is a Book of Remembrance containing the names of more than 18,000 of those members of 4 and 6 Groups who lost their lives, stationed on airfields around York between 1939 and 1945. Every year, four times a year, a contingent from RAF Linton-on-Ouse conducts a small ceremony to turn the pages of the Book of Remembrance.

Several Yorkshire squadron associations like those for 76 Squadron at Holme-on-Spalding Moor, for 578 Squadron at Burn, and for 51 Squadron at Snaith still flourish, and form opportunities for a dwindling band of veterans to meet and look back at those days when they were young and lived a fraught and dangerous life.

Looking at the process of remembering, there is the astonishing

example of the brothers Panton, Harold and Fred, of East Kirkby in Lincolnshire. As we have seen, they created a memorial to their elder brother P/O Christopher Panton, flight engineer in an aircraft flying from 6 Group in North Yorkshire, Skipton-on-Swale, who did not make it back from the infamous and costly Nuremberg raid of March 1944. East Kirkby is now a flourishing aviation museum, with hosts of visitors. You can pay to have taxiing rides round the airfield perimeter in the reconstituted Lancaster, *Just Jane,* which is a popular feature of this bustling enterprise. But this does not exhaust the measure and the depth of the Panton brothers' remembrance. Once a year one of the brothers makes a personal pilgrimage northwards to 6 Group country. He goes to the old airfield at Skipton-on-Swale, on the edge of the Yorkshire Dales, every year on the night of 30 March, the anniversary of his brother's departure for Nuremberg, and once there, pauses for a few moments of quiet reflection at the precise time of take-off. Memories of these hosts of young men, departed but not forgotten, cluster in these lonely places.

It seems appropriate to close with a poem about the strange life aircrew led, one night out with the girlfriend or wife, or a drink with the boys, the next night 20,000 ft up, or dead in some far corner of Europe. It's about a rear gunner, who was with Suzy one night and dead the next, by Roy Baum, a rear gunner in 10 Squadron at Melbourne near York, and it's called *Night Out:*

> Last night I was with Suzy,
> A kiss and cuddle for sure.
> Back seat at the Ritz, she's not choosy.
> But tonight I'm over the Ruhr.
> At the Ritz I'm her Errol Flynn,
> Though at first she'd play coy and pure;
> But now I've soared to a bigger sin
> In a turret over the Ruhr.
> Suzy is soft and warm to hold,
> Sighing love that's a cert to endure;
> Back of this kite I'm alone and cold
> In a mad sky over the Ruhr.
> And strangely I hear my Suzy say,
> 'The boy I loved, he just flew away'.

Index

Squadrons